Qualifikationsphase Sekundarstufe II

Pathway
Advanced

Mündliche Prüfung

Kopiervorlagen für die Kommunikationsprüfung
in der Qualifikationsphase

Herausgegeben von:
Iris Edelbrock

Erarbeitet von:
Franz Arnoldy
Yvonne von Detten
Sonja Kierdorf
Hans-Josef Speen

Sprachliche Betreuung:
Ronnie Halligan

 Schöningh

Begleitmaterialien zum Lehrwerk

Pathway Advanced Audio-CDs
4 CDs mit Hörtexten und Songs, Transkripte im Booklet
Best.-Nr. 062532-6

Pathway Advanced Skills and Language Trainer
Trainingsmaterial für Schülerinnen und Schüler
Best.-Nr. 040162-3

Pathway Advanced Abi kompakt
Thematic Vocabulary – Important Facts – Relevant Skills
Best.-Nr. 040164-7

Pathway Advanced Teachers' Manual
Best.-Nr. 040165-4

Pathway Advanced Comprehension
Reading – Listening – Viewing.
Kopiervorlagen mit standardisierten Aufgabenformaten
Best.-Nr. 040157-9

Pathway Advanced Klausurvorschläge
Vorschläge für Klausuren mit kombinierten Aufgabenformaten. Mit CD-ROM.
Best.-Nr. 040158-6

Pathway Advanced Mediation
Kopiervorlagen
Best.-Nr. 040163-0

© 2016 Bildungshaus Schulbuchverlage
Westermann Schroedel Diesterweg Schöningh Winklers GmbH
Braunschweig, Paderborn, Darmstadt

www.schoeningh-schulbuch.de
Schöningh Verlag, Jühenplatz 1 – 3, 33098 Paderborn

Auf verschiedenen Seiten dieses Buches befinden sich Verweise (Links) auf
Internetadressen. Haftungshinweis: Trotz sorgfältiger inhaltlicher Kontrolle wird
die Haftung für die Inhalte der externen Seiten ausgeschlossen. Für den Inhalt
dieser externen Seiten sind ausschließlich deren Betreiber verantwortlich.
Sollten Sie dabei auf kostenpflichtige, illegale oder anstößige Inhalte treffen, so
bedauern wir dies ausdrücklich und bitten Sie, uns umgehend per E-Mail davon
in Kenntnis zu setzen, damit beim Nachdruck der Verweis gelöscht wird.

Druck A 5 4 3 2 1 / Jahr 2020 19 18 17 16
Alle Drucke der Serie A sind im Unterricht parallel verwendbar.
Die letzte Zahl bezeichnet das Jahr dieses Druckes.

Umschlaggestaltung: Nora Krull, Bielefeld
Druck und Bindung: westermann druck GmbH, Braunschweig

ISBN 978-3-14-040159-3

Contents

Vorwort

Liebe Kollegin, lieber Kollege,

die vorliegende Sammlung von Materialien bietet Ihnen eine Auswahl von **Kopiervorlagen** für die Durchführung der mündlichen Prüfungen in der Qualifikationsphase 1 (Q1) der SII im Fach Englisch. Es handelt sich dabei um Kombinationen von Filmrezensionen (in gekürzter Fassung) und DVD-Covern, Auszügen aus politischen Reden und Cartoons, Artikel aus Zeitungen/Zeitschriften und Fotos und Romanauszügen und Stills/Bildmaterial aus Filmen sowie *role cards* mit den entsprechenden Aufgabenstellungen aus unterschiedlichen Themenfeldern.

Die verpflichtende Kommunikationsprüfung in der Q1 zielt auf die Kernkompetenz des **zusammenhängenden Sprechens** als auch die Kompetenz der **Teilnahme an Gesprächen** in thematischen Kontexten. Die Sprachprüfung ersetzt grundsätzlich eine Klausur bzw. kann modifiziert als Teil einer Klausur genutzt werden.

Die vorliegenden Materialien sind inhaltlich sowohl auf die Themenvorgaben der **Kernlehrpläne NRW** als auch auf Units des Schülerbuchs *Pathway Advanced* bezogen, aber auch unabhängig davon einsetzbar.

Folgende **Schwerpunkte** werden abgedeckt:
- Postcolonialism
  - Minorities
  - Diversity in Britain
- The American Dream
- Globalisation
- Science and Technology
  - Utopia & Dystopia

Damit entsprechen die thematischen Schwerpunkte vier Quartalen der Qualifikationsphase. Alternativ/ergänzend zur mündlichen Prüfung als Ersatz für eine Klausur können die Materialien als Übungsmaterial bzw. zur Leistungsüberprüfung im Unterricht, angebunden an den thematischen Kontext, eingesetzt werden.

Die Materialien sind ausgelegt für eine Kursgröße von max. 27 Schülern. Jedes Thema umfasst **neun Text- und Bildvorlagen** mit entsprechenden Aufgabenstellungen für die **Einzelprüfungen** plus **neun *role cards*** für die Gruppenprüfungen (zu jeweils 3 Schülern), die mit unterschiedlichen Einzelaspekten des Schwerpunktthemas korrespondieren.

Im Anhang des Heftes finden sich **Kopiervorlagen** zur Vorbereitung, Planung und Evaluierung der mündlichen Prüfung:
- Planungsbögen für Lehrer/Schüler/Schule für die Zeitkoordination der Prüfung(en)
- Bewertungsbogen für Lehrer
- Evaluationsbogen für Schüler
- Focus on Language: Communication and Discussion
- Focus on Skills: Oral Examination

Das Autorenteam

Methodische Hinweise und unterrichtliche Voraussetzungen zur Durchführung von mündlichen Prüfungen

Vorbereitung der Prüfungen

Die Schülerinnen und Schüler nehmen an den Prüfungstagen regulär am Unterricht teil und verlassen lediglich für die Zeitdauer ihrer Prüfung den betreffenden Unterricht. Über den **Aushang des Prüfungsplans** werden sie über die zeitliche Planung informiert.

Die Prüfungen werden von **zwei Lehrkräften** abgenommen, eine weitere Lehrkraft übernimmt die **Aufsicht im Vorbereitungsraum**.

Zur Vorbereitung sollten den Schülerinnen und Schülern **ein- und zweisprachige Wörterbücher** zur Verfügung gestellt werden.

Prüfungsorganisation und Vorbereitung des Schülervortrags

Wir schlagen vor, dass den Schülern ein Thema mit den entsprechenden Aufgaben aus dem Materialteil zum Oberthema sowie eine *role card* für das Gespräch im zweiten Teil der Prüfung zugewiesen wird.

Die **Vorbereitungszeit** für den ersten Teil der Prüfung beträgt ca. 20–25 Minuten (im Vorbereitungsraum). Die Höchstdauer der **Einzelvorträge beträgt 5 Minuten**. Der zweite Teil der Prüfung umfasst ca. 10–15 Minuten Gesprächszeit, je nachdem, ob Paar- oder Gruppenprüfungen vorgesehen sind.

Der **zweite Prüfungsteil umfasst ca. 10 Minuten** für eine Paarprüfung, bei einer Gruppenprüfung ca. 15 Minuten.

Im Hinblick auf die Organisation des Ablaufs der Prüfungen ist darauf zu achten, dass bei jeweils drei Schülergruppen à drei Schülern, die dieselben Materialien und Aufgaben

bearbeiten, die Schüler sich nicht „begegnen", d. h. – entsprechend einem Ablauf des mündlichen Abiturs – sich eine Schülergruppe im Prüfungsraum, eine weitere im Vorbereitungsraum befindet, während eine dritte Gruppe in den Vorbereitungsraum geleitet wird, bevor die erste Gruppe den Prüfungsraum verlässt, damit wechselseitige Hilfestellungen nicht gegeben werden können.

Je nach Gruppengröße des 2. Prüfungsteils (*communication skills*) muss der Zeitablauf für die Prüfungen neu abgestimmt werden.

Unterrichtliche Voraussetzungen

Topic	Reference Students' Book
1 Postcolonialism	
India	India: Democracy, Diversity and Determination ● The Raj – Britain's Dreams and India's Nightmares (pp. 112 – 123) ● 21st Century India (pp. 126 – 149)
Minorities and Multiculturalism in Britain	The U.K. Between Tradition and Modernity ● Once There Was … An Empire (pp. 45 – 60) ● The Commonwealth: Postcolonial Tasks & Challenges (pp. 84 – 89) ● Ethnic Communities in the U.K. – A Multicultural Kaleidoscope?! (pp. 91 – 104)
2 The American Dream/Nightmare	
	The American Dream – Reveries and Realities ● America and Americans – Inside and Outlooks (pp. 154 – 165) ● Founding and Shaping a Nation (pp. 167 – 178) ● The American Dream: "Opportunity for Each"? (pp. 181 – 189) ● When Dreams Go Bust (pp. 190 – 200) ● "Separate But Equal" (pp. 203 – 221) ● Minorities in the US (pp. 223 – 233) ● Dreams and Delusions (pp. 244 – 252)
3 Globalisation	
Migration	The World Going Global ● Migration and Outsourcing (pp. 290 – 301)
Climate Change	The World Going Global ● Environment vs. Resources (pp. 302 – 320)
The Economy/Cheap Labour	The World Going Global Global Trade and Consumption (pp. 325 – 337)
4 Science & Technology	
Scientific Developments	Towards a Better World?! ● Start-Up Activities (pp. 340 – 341) ● Genetic Engineering/Man between Molecules and Machines (pp. 342 – 362)
Utopia & Dystopia	Towards a Better World?! ● Between Euphoria and Disaster (pp. 365 – 372)

1a Minorities and Multiculturalism ▪ Team 1

PART 1: Presentation on the DVD Cover of *The Best Exotic Marigold Hotel*

1a Minorities and Multiculturalism ■ Team 1

PART 1: Presentation on the Film Review of *The Best Exotic Marigold Hotel*

"The Best Exotic Marigold Hotel" is a retirement destination in India for "the elderly and beautiful." It has seen better days, and if you want to see what the better days looked like, just examine the brochure, which depicts a luxurious existence in Udaipur, a popular tourist destination in Rajasthan. To this city travel a group of seven Brits with seven reasons for making the move — although the most urgent is that the local prices make retirement possible for them.

5 As we meet them jammed on the bus from the airport, we suspect that the film will be about their various problems and that the hotel will not be as advertised. What we may not expect is what a charming, funny and heart-warming movie this is, smoothly crafted entertainment that makes good use of seven superb veterans.

We're introduced to them while they're still at home in England. In the order of their billing, they are Evelyn Greenslade (Judi Dench), who has been forced to sell her London flat; [...]; Graham Dashwood (Tom Wilkinson), who spent

10 the happiest years of his life in India and has now returned to seek his young love [...].

Greeting them at the Best Exotic Marigold Hotel is its exuberant and optimistic owner, Sonny Kapoor (Dev Patel from "Slumdog Millionaire"). He has inherited the shabby inn from his late father and plans to run it himself, against the objections of his mother, who wants him to live with her in Delhi and marry the bride of her choice. Sonny has already picked out a bride himself – a girl who works in a call-outsourcing agency [...]

15 How can I suggest what a delight this film is? Let me try a little shorthand. Recall some of the wonderful performances you've seen from Judi Dench [...] and the others, and believe me when I say that this movie finds rich opportunities for all of them. Director John Madden ("Shakespeare in Love") has to juggle to keep his subplots in the air, but these actors are so distinctive, they do much of the work for him.

(340 words)

Reviewed by Roger Ebert on May 2, 2012, http://www.meetup.com/de/Fabulous-40-Plus-Womens-Social-Group/events/64889082/ [20.02.2016]

Your task »»

Briefly present the film at hand to your group members. Make use of the review as well as the DVD cover.

Analyse how the review and the cover manage to promote the film at hand.

1a Minorities and Multiculturalism ■ Team 2

PART 1: Presentation on the DVD Cover of *The Lunchbox*

1a Minorities and Multiculturalism ■ Team 2

PART 1: Presentation on the Film Review of *The Lunchbox*

"The Lunchbox" [is] the debut feature from Indian director Ritesh Batra. [...]
Through her cooking, middle-class Mumbai homemaker Ila (Nimrat Kaur) is looking to literally spice up her marriage to her distracted husband. She prepares delightful new dishes for him to eat at his workplace, conveying them via the dabbawallahs – lunchbox deliverymen, most of whom are illiterate, who, for 120 years, have fanned out across
5 the sprawling city on their bicycles. Mathematicians have studied their elaborate coding system that all but ensures that only one in a million lunchboxes will ever be delivered to the wrong address. "The Lunchbox" is about that one in a million.
The pleasantly shocked recipient of Ila's confections is Saajan (Irrfan Khan), a woebegone widower and government accountant who is planning to retire after 35 years of service. When his lunchbox, as is customary with the dabba-
10 wallahs, is returned to its sender, Ila is delighted to find its contents licked clean – until she coyly asks her husband how he liked the meal and realizes from his response the mistake. The two men apparently received each other's lunch.
Rather than correct the error, Ila persists in creating new dishes for her appreciative mystery man, including personal notes in the returned lunchboxes to which Saajan responds. Their relationship becomes an epistolary romance of
15 sorts. The question, of course, is, will they eventually meet?
[...] Batra captures well the crushing bustle of modern Mumbai and the ways in which Ila and Saajan, in their very different ways, are trapped by circumstance. We never see Ila outside her apartment, a gilded cage she shares with her husband and young daughter. Saajan's workplace is a drably lit office complex. We can certainly see why he wants out, although his home life is not much of a respite. After hours he smokes and dozes and watches old videos
20 of comedy shows his wife loved. There is no mystery in his life. He enjoys giving Ila advice about her troubles (he tells her that having another child might rescue her marriage), but he has no illusions about his own. [...]
(344 words)

Reviewed by Peter Rainer on February 28, 2014, http://www.csmonitor.com/The-Culture/Movies/2014/0228/The-Lunchbox-is-a-sweet-Mumbai-romance-deftly-directed-by-Ritesh-Batra [20.02.2016]

Your task »»»

Briefly present the film at hand to your group members. Make use of the review as well as the DVD cover.

Analyse how the review and cover manage to promote the film at hand.

1a Minorities and Multiculturalism ▪ Team 3

PART 1: Presentation on the DVD Cover of *Outsourced*

1a Minorities and Multiculturalism ■ Team 3

PART 1: Presentation on the Film Review of *Outsourced*

[…] Outsourced is sweet and light. It's a celebration of cultural diversity and an affirmation that, despite differences in race, religion, and societal norms, people are essentially the same, with a lack of understanding being a key block to better relations. […]

Todd (Josh Hamilton) is the manager of a call center for a novelty company based in Seattle. One day – seemingly no
5 different from any other – his world crumbles when his boss informs him that the entire department is being outsourced. Todd can keep his job, but there's a condition: he must travel to India to train his replacement and get the new call center's MPI (Minutes Per Incident) rate under 6.0. Reluctantly, Todd agrees to go. He doesn't relish leaving behind his comfortable home, but he fears the uncertainty of unemployment more. At first, he has trouble adjusting, but with the help of Puro (Asif Basra), the man he's training, and Asha (Ayesha Dharker), with whom he develops a
10 bond more intimate than friendship, he begins to acclimate to Indian society.

Outsourced is not overly jokey in the way it approaches Todd's cultural discomfort. There's humor to be found in these circumstances, as when a cow wanders into the call center and only Todd notices something unusual. […] Similar claims can be made about the movie's romance. Asha is engaged to be married (it's a union that was arranged when she was four years old), so there's no future in her relationship with Todd. They have a fling and, although their
15 feelings for one another are sincere, they are not destined to be together. This bittersweet component makes Outsourced seem better grounded in reality. […]

The film does not ignore the painful economic impacts caused by outsourcing and downsizing, but it finds new ways in which to address them. By taking Todd to India, Outsourced provides an opportunity to observe the situation from a different angle. This is a feel-good comedy, but there's truth to be mined beneath the lighthearted surface.

(330 words)

Reviewed by James Berardinelli in 2006, http://www.reelviews.net/reelviews/outsourced [20.02.2016]

Your task »»

> Briefly present the film at hand to your group members. Make use of the review as well as the DVD cover. Analyse how the review and cover manage to promote the film at hand.
>
> Then analyse the still and relate it to the excerpt.

1a Minorities and Multiculturalism

PART 2: Dialogue – Topic: The English Language in India

Role Card No. 2

Topic: The English Language in India

Situation:
You take part in a talk show on an Indian TV channel. The topic of the discussion is "The role of the English language in the process of India's rise to become a new superpower".

Your task:
You act now as the person below. Introduce yourself to the other persons you meet in the talk show.

Your role:

Name:	Hari Vishnu
From:	New Delhi
Age:	70
Education:	well-educated
Religion:	liberal Hindu
Interests:	The history of India from the British Raj to the present; appreciation of the new opportunities for young Indians that the future offers.

Role Card No. 1

Topic: The English Language in India

Situation:
You take part in a talk show on an Indian TV channel. The topic of the discussion is "The role of the English language in the process of India's rise to become a new superpower".

Your task:
You act now as the person below. Introduce yourself to the other persons you meet in the talk show.

Your role:

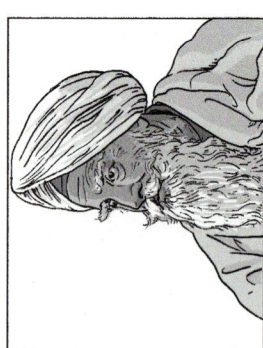

Name:	Bhagwan Patel
From:	Mumbai
Age:	64
Religion:	deeply religious Hindu
Interests:	Keeping up the traditional values, introducing Hindi as the one and only official language in India.

1a Minorities and Multiculturalism

PART 2: Dialogue – Topic: The English Language in India

Role Card No. 3

Topic: The English Language in India

Situation:

You take part in a talk show on an Indian TV channel. The topic of the discussion is "The role of the English language in the process of India's rise to become a new superpower".

Your task:

You act now as the person below. Introduce yourself to the other persons you meet in the talk show.

Your role:

Name:	Davinder Kaur
From:	Bangalore
Age:	35
Education:	well-educated, studied in the US
Religion:	Muslim
Interests:	The rise of the middle-class in India; supporter of women's rights in business, mentor for students interested in a career in the IT economy.

1b Minorities and Multiculturalism ■ Team 1

PART 1: Presentation on the DVD Cover of *Bend It Like Beckham*

1b Minorities and Multiculturalism ■ Team 1

PART 1: Presentation on the Film Review of *Bend It Like Beckham*

Bend It Like Beckham, directed by Gurinder tells the story of eighteen-year-old British-Asian Jess Bhamra (Parminder Nagra). She is a talented soccer player, and her idol is David Beckham, the star of Manchester United. One day, Jules (Keira Knightley), captain of the local women's team, comes across Jess who is playing football in the park. She introduces Jess to the club's young and charismatic coach Joe (Jonathan Rhys Meyers). Seeing her potential, he wants
5 her to go to Santa Clara, California, to become a professional football player. However, her traditionalist Sikh parents have other, more conventional plans for her future. [...]
Christian as well as South Asian theology expects youngsters to respect their elders and, consequently, the conventions, traditions, and moral assumptions they stand for. Jess breaks many rules in the process of carving out her own life. [... However,] Jess decides to respect her parents' feelings, and calls her football projects off. With her act, she al-
10 lows her father to show his wisdom and, ultimately, to set her free. So, the credo of the film is that a fruitful relationship between different generations presupposes the capacity for self-sacrifice, forgiveness and love. [...]
Mrs Bhamra warns Jess about being associated with Joe by pointing out the story of someone else who was expelled from the South Asian diasporic community because she had a relationship with a "gora." And when Jess's father tells his story of being "chased off like a dog" from the cricket grounds twenty years ago, and Jess replies that things have
15 changed and Hussein Nasser is now the chairman of the national team, her comment is dismissed by her mother who argues that Hussein does not count since he is a Muslim.
Bend It Like Beckham has been a huge success in Britain, and finds its place in the framework of the current enthusiastic reception of culturally diverse filmmaking. [...]
(303 words)
Reviewed by Béatrice Schatzmann-von Aesch on April 1, 2003, https://www.unomaha.edu/jrf/benditrev.htm [20.02.2016]

Your task ⫸

Briefly present the film at hand to your group members. Make use of the review as well as the DVD cover.

Analyse how the review and cover manage to promote the film at hand.

1b Minorities and Multiculturalism ▪ Team 2

PART 1: Presentation on the DVD Cover of *Bhaji on the Beach*

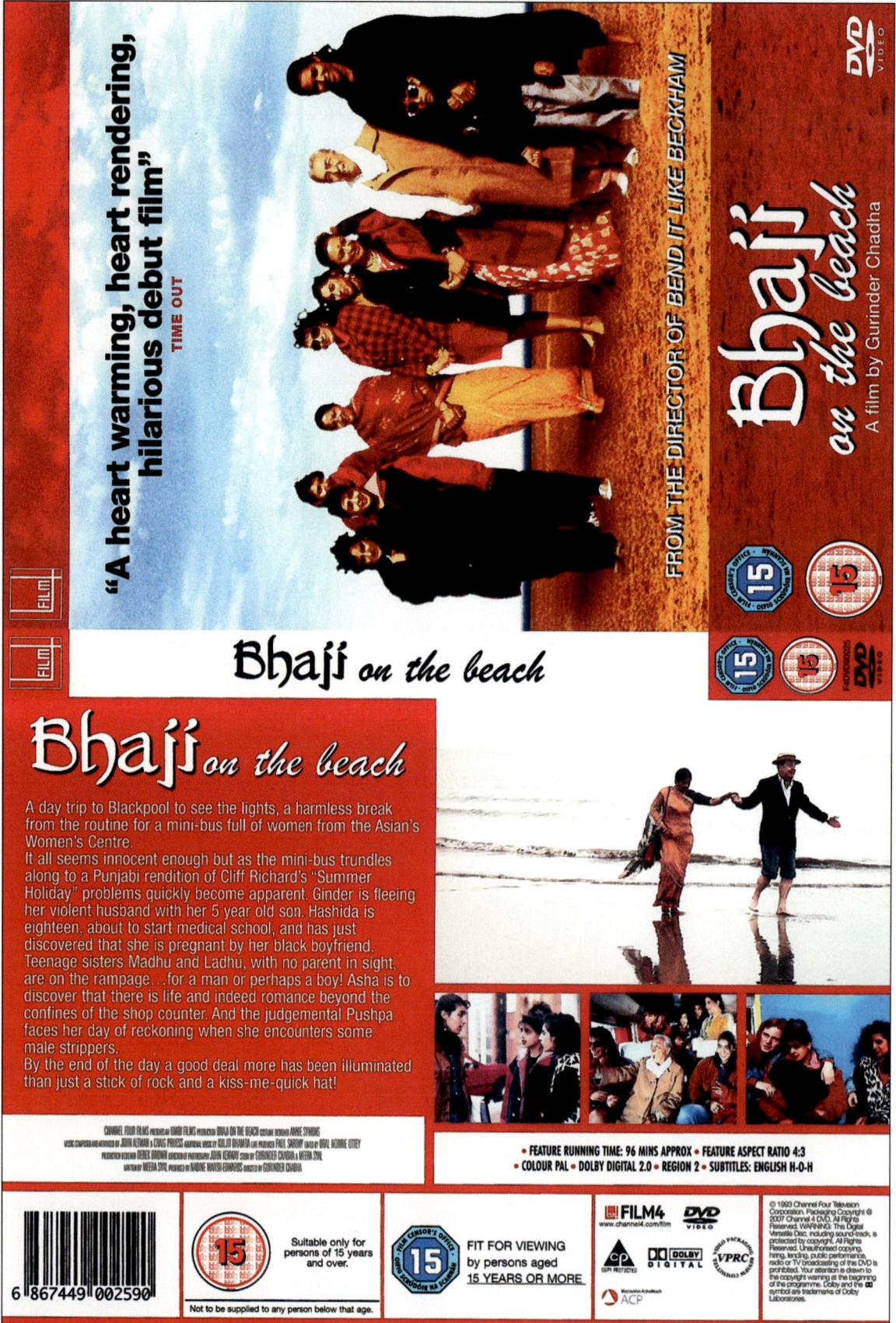

1b Minorities and Multiculturalism ■ Team 2

PART 1: Presentation on the Film Review of *Bhaji on the Beach*

"Bhaji on the Beach" is [... the] seriocomic story of a day trip to the seaside resort of Blackpool by several generations of women [...]. While "Bhaji's" key protagonists may sound just like the English they live among, they are separated from them not only by skin color but also by the difficulties of being a transitional generation, with one foot in the clannish, fearful society of their immigrant parents and the other in the modern Western world their futures will take

5 place in.

"Bhaji" begins in Birmingham, an industrial city in the Midlands, and its almost too-rapid introduction of characters gives audiences a sense of the crowded, hectic conditions of the Indian community there, with married children still living with their parents, and the whole business overseen by a network of vaguely related, invariably censorious older women known collectively [...] as aunties.

10 But by the time a bus holding a cross-section of women sets out for a day of "female fun" at Blackpool under the tutelage of feminist Simi, two of the passengers, each with her own romantic crisis, have come into focus as the film's parallel protagonists.

Ginder has precipitated a crisis in the close-knit community by leaving her husband, Ranjit, and moving into a women's shelter with her young son. And Hashida, a college graduate about to enter medical school, knows she will cause

15 even more of a sensation if word gets out that a) she is pregnant though unmarried and b) the father is a young black man of Caribbean descent named Oliver.

When the bus arrives at Blackpool, the city itself [...] becomes a character in the film. A place like this by definition encourages a loosening of bonds, allowing everyone from teenage sisters Ladhu and Madhu to decorous Auntie Asha to engage in amusing flirtations. And with both Ranjit and Oliver headed toward Blackpool to try to resolve their dif-

20 ficulties, more serious events are likely as well. [...]

(319 words)

Reviewed by Kenneth Turan on June 22, 1994, http://articles.latimes.com/1994-06-22/entertainment/ca-7049_1_gurinder-chadha [20.02.2016]

MOVIE REVIEW: 'Bhaji on the Beach' written by Kenneth Turan, June 22, 1994. Copyright © 1994. Los Angeles Times. Reprinted with permission.

Your task ⟫

> Briefly present the film at hand to your group members. Make use of the review as well as the DVD cover.
>
> Analyse how the review and cover manage to promote the film at hand.

1b Minorities and Multiculturalism ■ Team 3

PART 1: Presentation on the DVD Cover of *Brick Lane*

1b Minorities and Multiculturalism ▪ Team 3

PART 1: Presentation on the Film Review of *Brick Lane*

Nazneen lives with her parents and sisters in a rural Bangladesh village and has a close relationship with her sister Hasina. Growing up together, the girls are almost inseparable. Their mother always tells them that it is necessary to endure the hardships that life brings their way, but she herself cannot handle them and commits suicide. Nazneen's father decides to marry her off to Chanu (Satish Kaushik), an educated and older Muslim living in London's East End.
5 She is only 17 years old when she leaves the village.

Sixteen years later, Nazneen (Tannishtha Chatterjee) lives in Brick Lane, a rundown housing complex that is home to many immigrants. Having lost her first-born son in a crib death, she now has two daughters: Shahana (Naeema Begum), a rebellious teenager, and Bibi (Lana Rahman), a ten-year-old. Once her family leaves for the day, Nazneen eagerly reads a letter from her beloved sister about her adventures in love. She dreams of returning to Bangladesh, a
10 place which in her memories is idyllic in its beauty and security. Nazneen has never really accepted London as her home. Chanu returns home with bad news that after being passed over for a promotion, he has quit his job.

Although he protests at first, her husband allows Nazneen to set up a sewing business in their small apartment. A handsome young Bangladeshi man named Karim (Christopher Simpson) delivers the piece work for her to do. Initially she is very shy in his presence, but over time they talk and eventually become lovers. After 9/11, he is very active in
15 meetings with fellow Muslims who want to counter the hatred directed against them by people who are filled with fear. Nazneen faces new challenges at home. Chanu has borrowed a lot of money, and the old woman who loaned them the money is demanding exorbitant payments. Frustrated at every turn, her husband now wants to return to Bangladesh. Nazneen doesn't know what she wants but her oldest daughter is vehemently against the move. [...]
(331 words)

Your task ⟫

> Briefly present the film at hand to your group members. Make use of the review as well as the DVD cover.
>
> Analyse how the review and cover manage to promote the film at hand.

1b Minorities and Multiculturalism

PART 2: Dialogue – Topic: Arranged Marriages in India

Role Card No. 2

Topic: Arranged Marriages in India

Situation:

You take part in a talk show on an Indian TV channel. The topic of the discussion is "Should arranged marriages be abolished by law?".

Your task:

You act now as the person below. Introduce yourself to the other persons you meet in the talk show.

Your role:

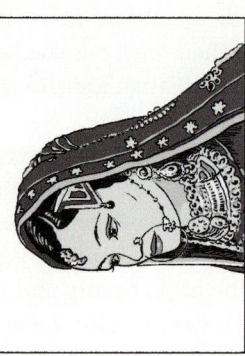

Name:	Amah Fariah, forced bride
From:	Madras
Age:	18
Religion:	Muslim
Education:	Higher education
Attitudes:	Against forced marriages, because she was told to marry the son of her parents' friends, a man she had never seen before; her brother threatened to kill her if she did not agree.

Role Card No. 1

Topic: Arranged Marriages in India

Situation:

You take part in a talk show on an Indian TV channel. The topic of the discussion is "Should arranged marriages be abolished by law?".

Your task:

You act now as the person below. Introduce yourself to the other persons you meet in the talk show.

Your role:

Name:	George Khan
From:	Kolkata
Age:	64
Religion:	Traditional Muslim
Attitudes:	Conservative father who is convinced that he is responsible for all the important decisions in the lives of his children. He thinks he knows what is best for his sons and daughters and wants to avoid disasters like a divorce.

1b Minorities and Multiculturalism

PART 2: Dialogue – Topic: Arranged Marriages in India

Role Card No. 3

Topic: Arranged Marriages in India

Situation:
You take part in a talk show on an Indian TV channel. The topic of the discussion is "Should arranged marriages be abolished by law?".

Your task:
You act now as the person below. Introduce yourself to the other persons you meet in the talk show.

Your role:

Name:	Jyoti Ambani
From:	Mumbai
Age:	39
Religion:	Muslim
Education:	University degree, businesswoman
Attitudes:	She is a very successful head of an international company who knows that young people today have a lot of rights that you have little control over; she wants to see her daughter happy and would not force her into a marriage, but she would try to influence her choice.

1c Minorities and Multiculturalism ■ Team 1

PART 1: Presentation on the DVD Cover of *Gandhi*

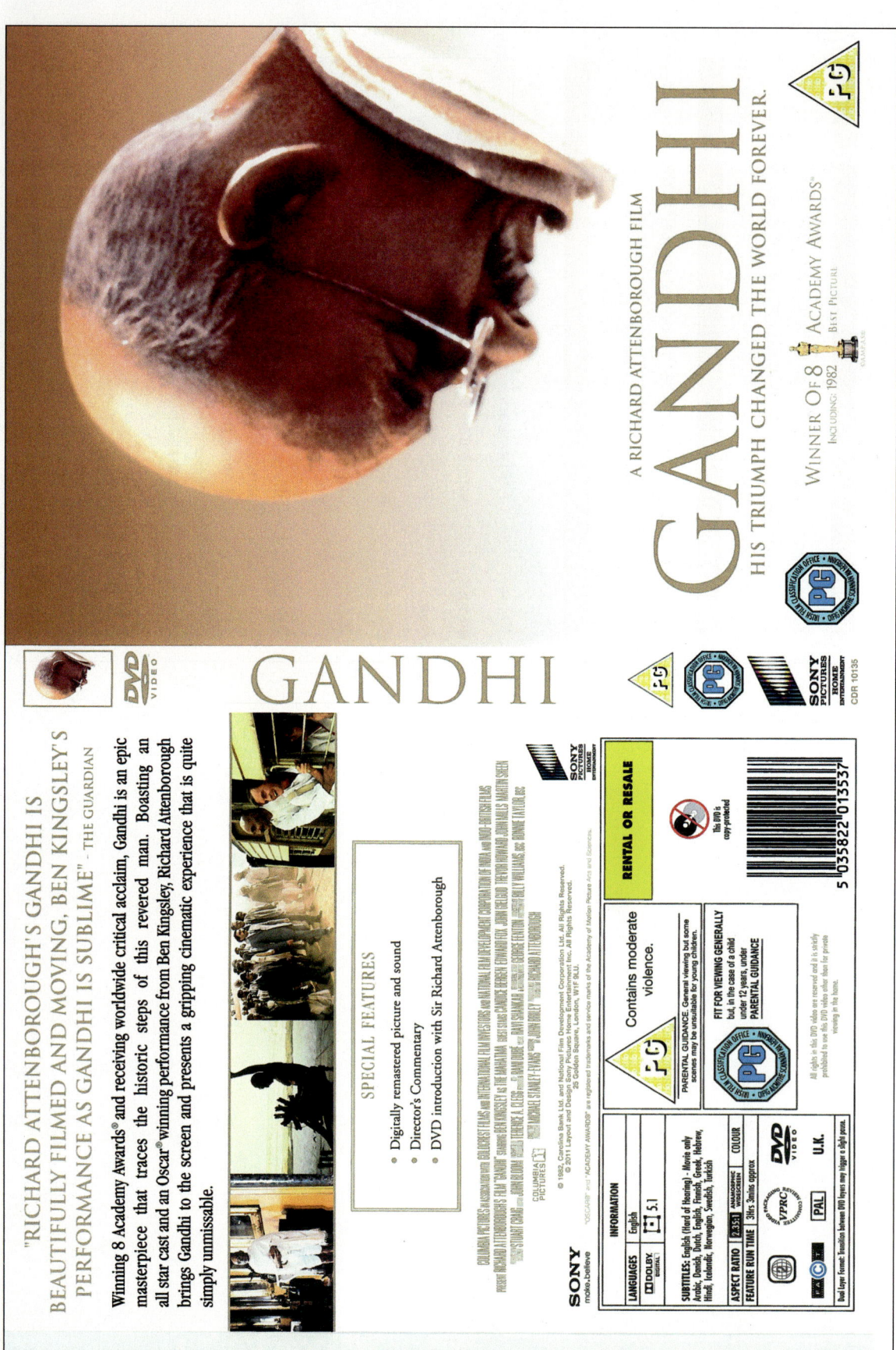

1c Minorities and Multiculturalism ▪ Team 1

PART 1: Presentation on the Film Review of *Gandhi*

[...] Richard Attenborough directed this massive epic about the man that freed India. The film opens with Gandhi's assassination. The next scene, his funeral, is one of the greatest scenes in cinematic history. Attenborough managed to recreate Gandhi's funeral on January 31ˢᵗ, 1981, the 33ʳᵈ anniversary of the actual funeral. It is estimated that nearly 400,000 people were on hand to be a part of the filming of the recreation. [...] The funeral scene is probably the last
5 live action crowd of this magnitude that will ever be filmed.

Mahatma Gandhi's message of non-violent resistance is delivered in an interesting and enthralling body of art. This film has made and will make millions of people aware of the little brown man that took on the British Empire and won. "Gandhi" serves both as entertainment and an important historical record of one of the most important figures in history.
10 Ben Kingsley played Gandhi. He was perfect for the role. He resembled the real Gandhi. He was young enough to portray Gandhi as a young man. He is a British actor who nailed the British-influenced Indian accent. He is a wonderful actor who was patient and humble despite playing such an important part. [...] He became Gandhi.

The cinematography was outstanding. Attenborough filmed "Gandhi" on location in India. The scenes of India are spectacular, and India is very much another character in the film. This film is as much about India itself as it is about
15 Gandhi. Attenborough shows the audience the people of India from its countryside to the vast city of Calcutta. [...] He persevered in enlisting thousands of Indians to help make this film. In every crowd scene, he used real Indians from the area. Attenborough also won both the Academy Award and Golden Globe for Best Direction.

This movie is a must-see for everyone. It should be required viewing in high schools, as part of the History class. The fight against prejudice will forever be relevant. It is also a beautiful work of art. [...]

(330 words)

Reviewed by 'Rod-88' from Dallas TX on January 29, 2002, http://www.imdb.com/title/tt0083987/reviews [20.02.2016]

Your task ⟫⟫

> Briefly present the film at hand to your group members. Make use of the review as well as the DVD cover.
>
> Analyse how the review and cover manage to promote the film at hand.

1c Minorities and Multiculturalism ■ Team 2

PART 1: Presentation on the DVD Cover of *A Passage to India*

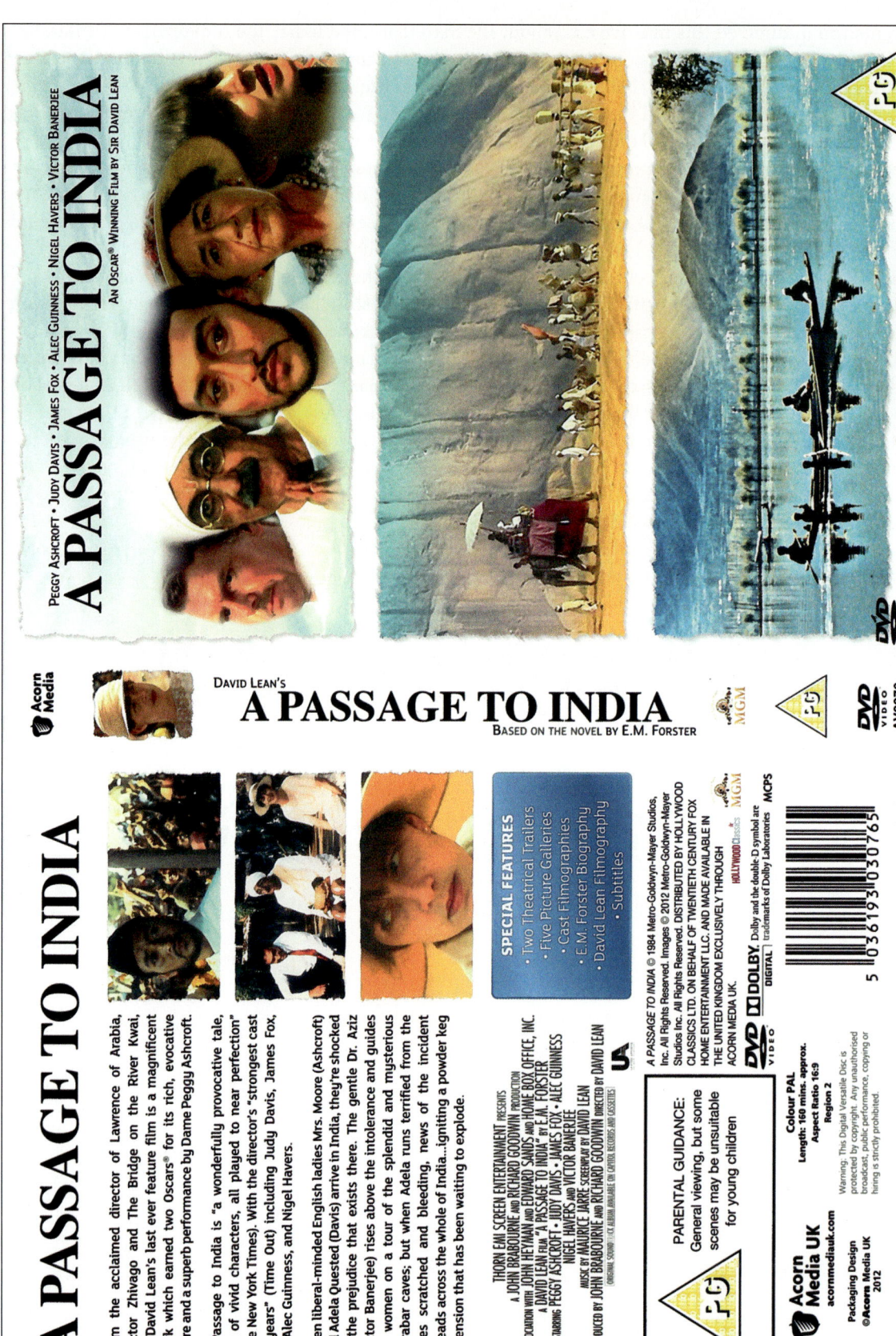

1c Minorities and Multiculturalism ▪ Team 2

PART 1: Presentation on the Film Review of *A Passage to India*

David Lean's film is [...] a film of epic quality, it follows two travelers on their journey from England to India during the Raj colonial period of the 1920s. For Adela Quested, it's her first time out of England to anywhere. For Mrs. Moore, it's a chance to visit her son, Ronny, who is expected to marry Adela during the visit. But, their visit is not without incident.

5 What both Adela and Mrs. Moore discover is an India ruled by British bureaucrats (Ronny being one of them, a city magistrate) who exude personal and cultural superiority over Indians. This is a shock to them since they both expected to find Indians and Britons meeting socially and on friendly terms. The only exception to that rule appears to be Fielding, principal of a college.

Through Fielding, Adela is introduced socially to Professor Godbole (a Hindu holy man) and Dr. Aziz (a Muslim phy-
10 sician). [...] During this social introduction, Aziz invites Mrs. Moore and Adela on a journey to the Marabar Caves, a tourist destination. During the trip, and tired from all the activity, Mrs. Moore stays at the encampment near the lower caves and encourages Aziz and Adela to explore the higher caves alone.

Then, something happens ... and I won't tell you what. Suffice it to say that Aziz finds himself in police custody. A court trial ensues that pits culture against culture, race against race, and clearly demonstrates the differences in at-
15 titudes between resident British citizens and Indians. But the climax of the trial isn't the most moving part of the film. Lean has raised the film's denouement to a higher level ... one that leaves you smiling and crying at the same time. [...]

In today's world, India is beset by inter-sect angst between Hindus, Muslims, Sikhs, and persons of other faiths. [...] It is perhaps a testament to the novelist (E.M. Forster) and Lean that they manage to show how British colonial rule
20 held rivalries in abeyance and to realize a potent underlying force in the story ... uniting Indians of all faiths into a common bond that eventually forced colonialism to end in India.

The film is a masterpiece on every level and remains one of my favourites of all time.

(338 words)

Reviewed by Alec West from the United States on November 24, 2005, http://www.imdb.com/title/tt0087892/reviews?ref_=tt_urv [20.02.2016]

Your task »»

Briefly present the film at hand to your group members. Make use of the review as well as the DVD cover.

Analyse how the review and cover manage to promote the film at hand.

1c Minorities and Multiculturalism ■ Team 3

PART 1: Presentation on the DVD Cover of *Midnight's Children*

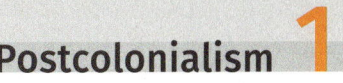
1c Minorities and Multiculturalism ▪ Team 3

PART 1: Presentation on the Film Review of *Midnight's Children*

Midnight's Children is a story about India after independence, and how the hopes for that country materialized for the first generation after 1947. But primarily this is a film about India. It is a sprawling, complex, epic movie with several themes, including Indian history, Indian politics, fate, destiny, the relationship between men and women, and social justice. The film tells us the life story of Saleem Sinai and his family. […]

5 The first half of the movie, the family drama involving the Sinai family, is the strongest. We follow the events that occur to this family, including the shocking act of two babies being switched at birth. We find out that our protagonist is not really from this family at all. The character development in this part of the movie is excellent. Some scenes from this part will remain with me a long time. About halfway through, the movie changes direction completely. I had to be dragged along after this because I was truly enjoying the family story and didn't want it to end. I feel it might have
10 been more satisfying to film this as two or three movies, rather than trying to cram it all into one.

Strange, supernatural and symbolic elements are added to the mix. […] I have to admit that this aspect did not work that well for me. I suppose it's because this film is mostly realistic, and I thought it was unnecessary.

At times I was quite moved, however, at other times I felt the pathos was laid on a little too thick. Also, some of the plot, and a few of the scenes, felt unrealistic to me, especially the portrayal of the military and war. […]
15 This is a movie that makes you think … […]

"India after independence did not turn out the way we wanted, but at least we survived." (But many did not.)

I would recommend this beautiful and passionate movie particularly to anyone who is interested in India and Salman Rushdie's work, and is willing to cope with the length, unevenness and stylized elements.

(341 words)

Reviewed by 'Laakbaar' from the Netherlands on June 9, 2013, http://www.imdb.com/title/tt1714866/reviews?ref_=tt_urv [20.02.2016]

Your task ⟫

> Briefly present the film at hand to your group members. Make use of the review as well as the DVD cover.
>
> Analyse how the review and cover manage to promote the film at hand.

1c Minorities and Multiculturalism

PART 2: Dialogue – Topic: Gandhi's Views

Role Card No. 2

Topic: Gandhi's Views

Situation:

You take part in a conference in London in 1946 whose task is to negotiate the independence of British India. The discussion circles around questions like "How can the process be solved non-violently?", "Should the people be active participants in the process?", "Should there be one country or a Hindu and a Muslim state in future?", "What form of government should be achieved?".

Your task:

You act now as the person below. Introduce yourself to the other persons you meet at the conference table.

Help:

Make use of all your knowledge about Indian history.

Your role:

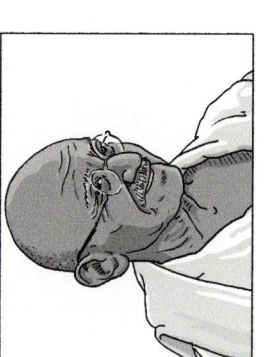

Name: Muhammad Ali Jinnah

Religion: Muslim

Attitudes/Aims: Leader of the Muslim community, fights for independence but also for a separate Muslim state which is to be later called Pakistan; in this aspect his opinion differs from that of Gandhi.

Role Card No. 1

Topic: Gandhi's Views

Situation:

You take part in a conference in London in 1946 whose task is to negotiate the independence of British India. The discussion circles around questions like "How can the process be solved non-violently?", "Should the people be active participants in the process?", "Should there be one country or a Hindu and a Muslim state in future?", "What form of government should be achieved?".

Your task:

You act now as the person below. Introduce yourself to the other persons you meet at the conference table.

Help:

Make use of all your knowledge about Indian history.

Your role:

Name: Mahatma Gandhi

Religion: Hindu

1c Minorities and Multiculturalism

PART 2: Dialogue – Topic: Gandhi's Views

Role Card No. 3

Topic: Gandhi's Views

Situation:

You take part in a conference in London in 1946 whose task is to negotiate the independence of British India. The discussion circles around questions like "How can the process be solved non-violently?", "Should the people be active participants in the process?", "Should there be one country or a Hindu and a Muslim state in future?", "What form of government should be achieved?".

Your task:

You act now as the person below. Introduce yourself to the other persons you meet at the conference table.

Help:

Make use of all your knowledge about Indian history.

Your role:

Name: Earl Louis Mountbatten

Religion: Anglican Church

Attitudes/Aims: His task is to prepare India's independence while protecting British interests and the security and well-being of the Indian population. His aim is to keep the peace and to see to a smooth transition.

1c Minorities and Multiculturalism

2a Challenges and Opportunities ■ Team 1

PART 1: Presentation on Immigration to the USA

George W. Bush
Address to the Nation on Immigration Reform

[...] The issue of immigration stirs intense emotions, and in recent weeks, Americans have seen those emotions on display. On the streets of major cities, crowds have rallied in support of those in our country illegally. At our southern border, others have organized to stop illegal immigrants from coming in. Across the country, Americans are trying to reconcile these contrasting images. And in Washington, the debate over immigration reform has reached a time of
5 decision. Tonight, I will make it clear where I stand, and where I want to lead our country on this vital issue.

We must begin by recognizing the problems with our immigration system. For decades, the United States has not been in complete control of its borders. As a result, many who want to work in our economy have been able to sneak across our border, and millions have stayed.

Once here, illegal immigrants live in the shadows of our society. Many use forged documents to get jobs, and that
10 makes it difficult for employers to verify that the workers they hire are legal. Illegal immigration puts pressure on public schools and hospitals, it strains state and local budgets, and brings crime to our communities. These are real problems. Yet we must remember that the vast majority of illegal immigrants are decent people who work hard, support their families, practice their faith, and lead responsible lives. They are a part of American life, but they are beyond the reach and protection of American law.

15 We're a nation of laws, and we must enforce our laws. We're also a nation of immigrants, and we must uphold that tradition, which has strengthened our country in so many ways. These are not contradictory goals. America can be a lawful society and a welcoming society at the same time. We will fix the problems created by illegal immigration, and we will deliver a system that is secure, orderly, and fair. So I support comprehensive immigration reform [...].
(325 words)

http://www.americanrhetoric.com/speeches/gwbimmigrationreform.htm, 15.05.2006 [15.02.2016]

Posted on 24/03/2010
by Signe Wilkinson

Your task ⟫⟫

Read the given excerpt. Sum up the content and point out the aspects related to the American Dream.

Then analyse the cartoon and compare it with the speech.

2a Challenges and Opportunities ■ Team 2

PART 1: Presentation on US Expansion to the Moon

John F. Kennedy
Moon Shot Speech to Congress

Fifty years ago, on May 25, 1961, President John F. Kennedy gave a historic speech before a joint session of Congress that set the United States on a course to the moon. This NASA-provided transcript shows the text of Kennedy's speech and what it called for, in 1961, to put Americans in space and on the moon before the decade ended. Just over eight years after the speech, on July 20, 1969, NASA's Apollo 11 mission would land the first humans on the moon.

Since early in my term, our efforts in space have been under review. With the advice of the Vice President, who is Chairman of the National Space Council, we have examined where we are strong and where we are not, where we may succeed and where we may not. Now it is time to take longer strides – time for a great new American enterprise – time for this nation to take a clearly leading role in space achievement, which in many ways may hold the key to
5 our future on earth. [...]
For while we cannot guarantee that we shall one day be first, we can guarantee that any failure to make this effort will make us last. [...] But this is not merely a race. Space is open to us now; and our eagerness to share its meaning is not governed by the efforts of others. We go into space because whatever mankind must undertake, free men must fully share. [...]
10 I believe that this nation should commit itself to achieving the goal, before this decade is out, of landing a man on the moon and returning him safely to the Earth. No single space project in this period will be more impressive to mankind, or more important for the long-range exploration of space; and none will be so difficult or expensive to accomplish. [...]
It is a most important decision that we make as a nation. But all of you have lived through the last four years and have
15 seen the significance of space and the adventures in space, and no one can predict with certainty what the ultimate meaning will be of mastery of space.
I believe we should go to the moon. [...]
New objectives and new money cannot solve these problems. They could in fact, aggravate them further – unless every scientist, every engineer, every serviceman, every technician, contractor, and civil servant gives his personal
20 pledge that this nation will move forward, with the full speed of freedom, in the exciting adventure of space.
(332 words)

http://www.americanrhetoric.com/speeches/gwbush911addresstothenation.htm, 25.05.1961 [15.02.2016]

Posted on 16/07/2009
by Joe Heller

Your task »»»

Read the given excerpt. Sum up the content and point out the aspects related to the American Dream.

Then analyse the cartoon and compare it with the speech.

2a Challenges and Opportunities ■ Team 3

PART 1: Presentation on the Divide of Race in the USA

Bill Clinton
Second Inaugural Address

My fellow citizens:
At this last presidential inauguration of the 20th century, let us lift our eyes toward the challenges that await us in the next century. [...]

The promise of America was born in the 18th century out of the bold conviction that we are all created equal. It was
5 extended and preserved in the 19th century, when our nation spread across the continent, saved the union, and abolished the awful scourge of slavery. [...]

Americans produced a great middle class and security in old age; built unrivaled centers of learning and opened public schools to all; split the atom and explored the heavens; invented the computer and the microchip; and deepened the wellspring of justice by making a revolution in civil rights for African Americans and all minorities, and extend-
10 ing the circle of citizenship, opportunity and dignity to women. [...]

Our greatest responsibility is to embrace a new spirit of community for a new century. For any one of us to succeed, we must succeed as one America.

The challenge of our past remains the challenge of our future – will we be one nation, one people, with one common destiny, or not? Will we all come together, or come apart?
15 The divide of race has been America's constant curse. And each new wave of immigrants gives new targets to old prejudices. Prejudice and contempt, cloaked in the pretense of religious or political conviction are no different. These forces have nearly destroyed our nation in the past. They plague us still. They fuel the fanaticism of terror. And they torment the lives of millions in fractured nations all around the world. [...]

From the height of this place and the summit of this century, let us go forth. May God strengthen our hands for the
20 good work ahead – and always, always bless our America.

(305 words)

http://www.thisnation.com/library/inaugural/clinton2.html, 20.01.1997 [15.02.2016]

"THE TALK"

WHITE AMERICANS | AFRICAN-AMERICANS

U.S. JUSTICE SYSTEM

Posted on 16/07/2013
by Steve Sack

Your task ≫

Read the given excerpt. Sum up the content and point out the aspects related to the American Dream.

Then analyse the cartoon and compare it with the speech.

2a Challenges and Opportunities

PART 2: Dialogue – Topic: Immigration to the US

Role Card No. 2

Topic: Immigration to the US

Situation:

You take part in a late night TV show in the US. The topic of the discussion is "Should illegal immigrants be arrested and sent back to their home countries?" .

Your task:

You act now as the person below. Introduce yourself to the other persons you meet in the show.

Your role:

Name:	Virginia Steffens
From:	Phoenix, Arizona
Age:	66
Profession:	retired school-bus driver
Attitude:	Opposes illegal immigration on the ground that illegal immigrants only take advantage of the American social and economic system.

Role Card No. 1

Topic: Immigration to the US

Situation:

You take part in a late night TV show in the US. The topic of the discussion is "Should illegal immigrants be arrested and sent back to their home countries?"

Your task:

You act now as the person below. Introduce yourself to the other persons you meet in the show.

Your role:

Name:	Walter Hammersmith
From:	Santa Barbara, California
Age:	54
Profession:	farmer
Attitude:	Regularly employs illegal immigrants, because he cannot get other cheap workers to work in the fields.

2a Challenges and Opportunities

PART 2: Dialogue – Topic: Immigration to the US

Role Card No. 3

Topic: Immigration to the US

Situation:

You take part in a late night TV show in the US. The topic of the discussion is "Should illegal immigrants be arrested and sent back to their home countries?"

Your task:

You act now as the person below. Introduce yourself to the other persons you meet in the show.

Your role:

Name:	Hoa Lei
From:	Washington D.C. (originally from Vietnam)
Age:	48
Profession:	barkeeper
Attitude:	Came to the US as a legal immigrant in the 80s and is in favour of giving others the chance she had.

2b Changes and Challenges ■ Team 1

PART 1: Presentation on Obama's Encouraging Remarks to the Nation

Barack Obama
Speech in New Hampshire

[...] In the unlikely story that is America, there has never been anything false about hope. For when we have faced down impossible odds; when we've been told that we're not ready, or that we shouldn't try, or that we can't, generations of Americans have responded with a simple creed that sums up the spirit of a people. Yes we can.

It was a creed written into the founding documents that declared the destiny of a nation. Yes we can.

5 It was whispered by slaves and abolitionists as they blazed a trail toward freedom through the darkest of nights. Yes we can.

It was sung by immigrants as they struck out from distant shores and pioneers who pushed westward against an unforgiving wilderness. Yes we can.

It was the call of workers who organized; women who reached for the ballot; a President who chose the moon as our

10 new frontier; and a King who took us to the mountaintop and pointed the way to the Promised Land.

Yes we can to justice and equality. Yes we can to opportunity and prosperity. Yes we can heal this nation. Yes we can repair this world. Yes we can.

And so tomorrow, as we take this campaign South and West; as we learn that the struggles of the textile worker in Spartanburg are not so different than the plight of the dishwasher in Las Vegas; that the hopes of the little girl who

15 goes to a crumbling school in Dillon are the same as the dreams of the boy who learns on the streets of LA; we will remember that there is something happening in America; that we are not as divided as our politics suggests; that we are one people; we are one nation; and together, we will begin the next great chapter in America's story with three words that will ring from coast to coast; from sea to shining sea – Yes. We. Can.

(322 words)

https://www.nwprogressive.org/weblog/2008/01/barack-obamas-speech-in-new-hampshire.html, 08.01.2008 [15.02.2016]

Posted on 05/06/2013
by Zapiro

Your task »»

Read the given excerpt. Sum up the content and point out the aspects related to the American Dream.

Then analyse the cartoon and compare it with the speech.

2b Changes and Challenges ■ Team 2

PART 1: Presentation on the Nation's Space Efforts

John F. Kennedy
We Choose to Go to the Moon

It was one of Kennedy's earlier speeches meant to persuade the American people to support the national effort to land a man on the Moon and return him safely to the Earth.

We set sail on this new sea because there is new knowledge to be gained, and new rights to be won, and they must be won and used for the progress of all people. For space science, like nuclear science and all technology, has no conscience of its own. Whether it will become a force for good or ill depends on man, and only if the United States occupies a position of pre-eminence can we help decide whether this new ocean will be a sea of peace or a new terrifying
5 theater of war. I do not say that we should or will go unprotected against the hostile misuse of space any more than we go unprotected against the hostile use of land or sea, but I do say that space can be explored and mastered without feeding the fires of war, without repeating the mistakes that man has made in extending his writ around this globe of ours.

There is no strife, no prejudice, no national conflict in outer space as yet. Its hazards are hostile to us all. Its conquest
10 deserves the best of all mankind, and its opportunity for peaceful cooperation may never come again. But why, some say, the Moon? Why choose this as our goal? And they may well ask, why climb the highest mountain? Why, 35 years ago, fly the Atlantic? Why does Rice play Texas?

We choose to go to the Moon! … We choose to go to the Moon in this decade and do the other things, not because they are easy, but because they are hard; because that goal will serve to organize and measure the best of our energies
15 and skills, because that challenge is one that we are willing to accept, one we are unwilling to postpone, and one we intend to win …

(305 words)

http://er.jsc.nasa.gov/seh/ricetalk.htm, 12.09.1962 [01.03.2016]

Posted on 10/10/2009 by Tom Johnston

Your task »»»

Read the given excerpt. Sum up the content and point out the aspects related to the American Dream.

Then analyse the cartoon and compare it with the speech.

2b Changes and Challenges ■ Team 3

PART 1: Presentation on Reagan's Commencement of the Second Four-Year Term

Ronald Reagan
Second Inaugural Address

Senator Mathias, Chief Justice Burger, Vice President Bush, Speaker O'Neill, Senator Dole, Reverend Clergy, members of my family and friends, and my fellow citizens: [...]

There is only one way safely and legitimately to reduce the cost of national security, and that is to reduce the need for it. And this we are trying to do in negotiations with the Soviet Union. We are not just discussing limits on a further

5 increase of nuclear weapons. We seek, instead, to reduce their number. We seek the total elimination one day of nuclear weapons from the face of the Earth.

Now, for decades, we and the Soviets have lived under the threat of mutual assured destruction; if either resorted to the use of nuclear weapons, the other could retaliate and destroy the one who had started it. Is there either logic or morality in believing that if one side threatens to kill tens of millions of our people, our only recourse is to threaten

10 killing tens of millions of theirs?

I have approved a research program to find, if we can, a security shield that would destroy nuclear missiles before they reach their target. It wouldn't kill people, it would destroy weapons. It wouldn't militarize space, it would help demilitarize the arsenals of Earth. It would render nuclear weapons obsolete. We will meet with the Soviets, hoping that we can agree on a way to rid the world of the threat of nuclear destruction.

15 We strive for peace and security, heartened by the changes all around us. Since the turn of the century, the number of democracies in the world has grown fourfold. Human freedom is on the march, and nowhere more so than our own hemisphere. Freedom is one of the deepest and noblest aspirations of the human spirit. People, worldwide, hunger for the right of self-determination, for those inalienable rights that make for human dignity and progress.

[...] God bless you and may God bless America.

(324 words)

http://www.bartleby.com/124/pres62.html, 21.01.1985 [15.02.2016]

Posted on 16/01/2010
by DER

Your task ⟫⟫

Read the given excerpt. Sum up the content and point out the aspects related to the American Dream.

Then analyse the cartoon and compare it with the speech.

2b Changes and Challenges

PART 2: Dialogue – Topic: Minorities/Equal Rights

Role Card No. 2

Topic: Minorities/Equal Rights

Situation:
You take part in a late night TV show in the US. The topic of the discussion is "Does everybody in the US have equal rights?".

Your task:
You act now as the person below. Introduce yourself to the other persons you meet in the show.

Your role:

Name:	Joe Allen
From:	Charleston, South Carolina
Age:	57
Profession:	pastor
Attitude:	Works for equal rights carrying on the traditions of Martin Luther King, defending black people who have been treated unjustly by police authorities.

Role Card No. 1

Topic: Minorities/Equal Rights

Situation:
You take part in a late night TV show in the US. The topic of the discussion is "Does everybody in the US have equal rights?".

Your task:
You act now as the person below. Introduce yourself to the other persons you meet in the show.

Your role:

Name:	Debbie Galvin
From:	New York City
Age:	35
Profession:	police officer
Attitude:	Feels threatened in confrontations with young African-American and Latino males.

2b Changes and Challenges

PART 2: Dialogue – Topic: Minorities/Equal Rights

Role Card No. 3

Topic: Minorities/Equal Rights

Situation:

You take part in a late night TV show in the US. The topic of the discussion is "Does everybody in the US have equal rights?".

Your task:

You act now as the person below. Introduce yourself to the other persons you meet in the show.

Your role:

Name:	Ernestina Suarez, illegal immigrant
From:	Texas, originally from Mexico
Age:	21
Profession:	occasional jobs for local farmers
Attitude:	Frustrated but still hopes to find a regular well-paid job and to have the chance of becoming a regular US citizen.

2c War and Prayer ■ Team 1

PART 1: Presentation on the Response to the Attacks on the World Trade Center

Rudolph W. Giuliani
Speech at the Citywide Prayer Service

On September 11th, New York City suffered the darkest day in our history. It is now up to us to make this our finest hour.

Today we come together in the Capital of the World, as a united City. We're accompanied by religious leaders of every faith, to offer a prayer for the families of those who have been lost … to offer a prayer for our City … and to offer a
5 prayer for America.

The proud Twin Towers that once crowned our famous skyline – no longer stand. But our skyline will rise again.

In the words of President George W. Bush, "we will rebuild New York City."

To those who say that our City will never be the same, I say you are right. It will be better.

Now we understand much more clearly why people from all over the globe want to come to New York, and to Ameri-
10 ca … why they always have, and why they always will.

It's called freedom, equal protection under law, respect for human life, and the promise of opportunity.

All of the victims of this tragedy were innocent.

All of them were heroes. […]

In the days since this attack, we have met the worst of humanity with the best of humanity.

15 We pray for our President, George W. Bush … and for our Governor George Pataki … who have provided us with such inspiring leadership during these very, very difficult times. We pray for all of those whose loved ones are lost or missing … we pray for our children, and we say to them: "Do not be afraid. It's safe to live your life." Finally, we pray for America … and for all of those who join us in defending freedom, law, and humanity.

We humbly bow our heads and we ask God to bless the City of New York, and we ask God to bless the United States
20 of America.

Thank you.

(327 words)

http://www.nyc.gov/html/records/rwg/html/2001b/prayer_service.html, 23.09.2001 [15.02.2016]

Posted on 11/09/2011
by Mike Ritter

STILL STANDING

Your task »»»

Read the given excerpt. Sum up the content and point out the aspects related to the American Dream.

Then analyse the cartoon and compare it with the speech.

2c War and Prayer ■ Team 2

PART 1: Presentation on the Terrorist Attacks on the World Trade Center

George W. Bush
A Great People Has Been Moved to Defend a Great Nation

Good evening.

Today, our fellow citizens, our way of life, our very freedom came under attack in a series of deliberate and deadly terrorist acts. The victims were in airplanes or in their offices: secretaries, business men and women, military and federal workers, moms and dads, friends and neighbors. Thousands of lives were suddenly ended by evil, despicable acts
5 of terror. The pictures of airplanes flying into buildings, fires burning, huge – huge structures collapsing have filled us with disbelief, terrible sadness, and a quiet, unyielding anger. These acts of mass murder were intended to frighten our nation into chaos and retreat. But they have failed. Our country is strong.

A great people has been moved to defend a great nation. Terrorist attacks can shake the foundations of our biggest buildings, but they cannot touch the foundation of America. These acts shatter steel, but they cannot dent the steel of
10 American resolve. America was targeted for attack because we're the brightest beacon for freedom and opportunity in the world. And no one will keep that light from shining. Today, our nation saw evil – the very worst of human nature – and we responded with the best of America. With the daring of our rescue workers, with the caring for strangers and neighbors who came to give blood and help in any way they could. [...]

Tonight, I ask for your prayers for all those who grieve, for the children whose worlds have been shattered, for all
15 whose sense of safety and security has been threatened. [...]

This is a day when all Americans from every walk of life unite in our resolve for justice and peace. America has stood down enemies before, and we will do so this time. None of us will ever forget this day, yet we go forward to defend freedom and all that is good and just in our world.

Thank you. Good night. And God bless America.

(321 words)

http://www.americanrhetoric.com/speeches/gwbush911addresstothenation.htm, 11.09.2001 [15.02.2016]

America returns

Posted on 08/09/2011
by Bill Day

Your task »»

Read the given excerpt. Sum up the content and point out the aspects related to the American Dream.

Then analyse the cartoon and compare it with the speech.

2c War and Prayer ■ Team 3

PART 1: Presentation on Previous Foreign Policy Remarks Concerning the Promotion of Democracy Around the World

George W. Bush
Second Inaugural Address

Vice President Cheney, Mr. Chief Justice, President Carter, President Bush, President Clinton, reverend clergy, distinguished guests, fellow citizens:

[...] We have seen our vulnerability – and we have seen its deepest source. For as long as whole regions of the world simmer in resentment and tyranny – prone to ideologies that feed hatred and excuse murder – violence will gather,
5 and multiply in destructive power, and cross the most defended borders, and raise a mortal threat. There is only one force of history that can break the reign of hatred and resentment, and expose the pretensions of tyrants, and reward the hopes of the decent and tolerant, and that is the force of human freedom.

We are led, by events and common sense, to one conclusion: The survival of liberty in our land increasingly depends on the success of liberty in other lands. The best hope for peace in our world is the expansion of freedom in all the
10 world.

America's vital interests and our deepest beliefs are now one. From the day of our Founding, we have proclaimed that every man and woman on this earth has rights, and dignity, and matchless value, because they bear the image of the Maker of Heaven and Earth. Across the generations we have proclaimed the imperative of self-government, because no one is fit to be a master, and no one deserves to be a slave. Advancing these ideals is the mission that created our
15 Nation. It is the honorable achievement of our fathers. Now it is the urgent requirement of our nation's security, and the calling of our time.

So it is the policy of the United States to seek and support the growth of democratic movements and institutions in every nation and culture, with the ultimate goal of ending tyranny in our world. [...]

America's influence is not unlimited, but fortunately for the oppressed, America's influence is considerable, and we
20 will use it confidently in freedom's cause.

(324 words)

http://www.npr.org/templates/story/story.php?storyId=4460172, 20.01.2005 [15.02.2016]

Posted on 18/11/2007
by Mike Keefe

Your task »»

Read the given excerpt. Sum up the content and point out the aspects related to the American Dream.

Then analyse the cartoon and compare it with the speech.

2c War and Prayer

PART 2: Dialogue – Topic: The Frontier

Role Card No. 2

Topic: The Frontier

Situation:

You take part in a panel discussion. The topic of the discussion is "The Frontier and unlimited possibilities in the US: historical perspectives and future developments".

Your task:

You act now as the person below. Introduce yourself to the other persons you meet in the show.

Your role:

Name:	Arnold Schwarzenegger
From:	Los Angeles, California, originally from Austria
Age:	68
Profession:	actor, ex-governor of California, ex-bodybuilder
Attitude:	Everybody has the chance to fulfil his dreams in the US.

Role Card No. 1

Topic: The Frontier

Situation:

You take part in a panel discussion. The topic of the discussion is "The Frontier and unlimited possibilities in the US: historical perspectives and future developments".

Your task:

You act now as the person below. Introduce yourself to the other persons you meet in the show.

Your role:

Name:	Buzz Aldrin
From:	Montclair, New Jersey
Age:	84
Profession:	member of the first crew to land on the moon together with Neil Armstrong
Attitude:	Believes that the realisation of individual opportunities is not only a step for a man, but may also be "a giant leap for mankind" (Neil Armstrong).

2c War and Prayer

PART 2: Dialogue – Topic: The Frontier

Role Card No. 3

Topic: The Frontier

Situation:

You take part in a panel discussion. The topic of the discussion is "The Frontier and unlimited possibilities in the US: historical perspectives and future developments".

Your task:

You act now as the person below. Introduce yourself to the other persons you meet in the show.

Your role:

Name:	Major Michael Davis O'Donnell
From:	Frankfort, Kentucky
Age:	62
Profession:	war veteran without job, as he returned disabled from the Vietnam War
Attitude:	Went to Vietnam to fight for freedom and democracy, but returned completely disillusioned after experiencing all sorts of horrible cruelties and seeing his entire platoon wiped out.

3a Global Trade, Modern Slavery and Migration ▪ Team 1

PART 1: Presentation on Bangladesh Workers Suffering from Poor Conditions

Jason Burke
Bangladesh Garment Workers Suffer Poor Conditions Two Years After Reform

Assault, verbal abuse and forced overtime persist following the Rana Plaza disaster, which killed 1,100 people in Dhaka, Human Rights Watch claims.

Workers in factories in Bangladesh making clothes for western firms continue to suffer from poor working conditions two years after a factory collapse that killed 1,100 people and prompted widespread promises of reforms, a new report by campaigners claims.

The report from Human Rights Watch, the independent advocacy organisation, comes on the second anniversary of
5 the collapse of the Rana Plaza factory on the outskirts of Dhaka, the capital of Bangladesh.

More than 1,100 garment workers working on orders for high-street retailers in the west died in the tragedy, which briefly focused global attention on the problems created by the booming global clothing industry.

Following the disaster, retailers and Bangladesh's government promised widespread reforms. Thousands of factories have since been checked for structural problems with dozens closed and others refurbished, and many more helped
10 to improve working conditions and treatment of employees in initiatives partly paid for by western retailers. However, the report suggests problems remain.

Researchers [...] heard complaints of physical assault, verbal abuse, forced overtime, unsanitary conditions, denial of paid maternity leave, and failure to pay wages and bonuses on time or in full. [...]

The clothing industry in Bangladesh is second only to China's in size and employs about four million people, mainly
15 women, in approximately 3,500 factories. Ready-made garments account for nearly four-fifths of the country's exports and contributes more than 10% of GDP of the developing south Asian nation. [...]

Phil Robertson, Asia deputy director at Human Rights Watch, said: "If Bangladesh wants to avoid another Rana Plaza disaster, it needs to effectively enforce its labour law and ensure that garment workers enjoy the right to voice their concerns about safety and working conditions without fear of retaliation or dismissal." [...]

20 However, the Human Rights Watch report acknowledges the role played by the garments industry in the economic development of Bangladesh. "Continuing the economic success of the Bangladesh garment sector offers benefits for everyone – the retail companies and their consumers, factory owners, and the government ... But those gains should not come at the cost of lives and the suffering of garment workers struggling for a better future," it said.

(351 words)

The Guardian, 22 April 2015

A collapsed garment factory in Bangladesh

Your task ⫸

Read the given article. Sum up the content and point out the aspects related to globalisation.

Then analyse the photo and compare it with the article.

3a Global Trade, Modern Slavery and Migration ■ Team 2

PART 1: Presentation on Exploitation in the Chocolate Industry

Christian Parenti
Chocolate's Bittersweet Economy

Outside the village of Sinikosson in southwestern Ivory Coast, along a trail tracing the edge of a muddy fishpond, Madi Ouedraogo sits on the ground picking up cocoa pods[1] in one hand, hacking them open with a machete in the other and scooping[2] the filmy white beans into plastic buckets. It is the middle of the school day, but Madi, who looks to be about 10, says his family can't afford the fees to send him to the nearest school, five miles away. "I don't like this
5 work," he says. "I would rather do something else. But I have to do this."

Sinikosson, accessible only by rutted[3] jungle tracks, is a long way from the luxurious chocolate shops of New York and Paris. But it is here, on small West African farms like these, that 70 percent of the world's cocoa beans are grown – 40 percent from just one country, Ivory Coast. It's not only the landscape that is tough. Working and living conditions are brutal. Most villages lack electricity, running water, health clinics or schools. And to make ends meet,
10 underage cocoa workers, like Madi and the two boys next to him, spend their days wielding machetes, handling pesticides and carrying heavy loads.

This type of child labor isn't supposed to exist in Ivory Coast. Not only is it explicitly barred[4] by law – the official working age in the country is 18 – but since the issue first became public seven years ago, there has been an international campaign by the chocolate industry, governments and human rights organizations to eradicate the problem.
15 Yet today child workers, many under the age of 10, are everywhere. [...]

A more effective way to combat[5] child labor would be for the government of Ivory Coast to invest some of the revenue[6] it gets from high taxes on cocoa exporters in education and social services to help poor farmers. But the government of Ivory Coast is ranked among the most corrupt in the world by Transparency International, a nongovernmental watchdog group. And it seems happier making excuses than changes.

(346 words)

Fortune, 15 February 2008

---

[1] **pod** *Hülse, Schote* – [2] **to scoop sth.** *etwas löffeln* – [3] **rutted** *durchfurcht, ausgefahren* – [4] **barred** *verboten, untersagt* – [5] **to combat** *etwas bekämpfen* – [6] **revenue** *Erträge, Einkünfte*

Graffito "Rickshaw Kid" by Banksy, an English artist, political activist and film director whose real identity is unknown

Your task ⟫

Read the given article. Sum up the content and point out the aspects related to globalisation.

Then analyse the graffito and compare it with the article.

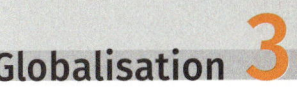

3a Global Trade, Modern Slavery and Migration ▪ Team 3

PART 1: Presentation on Europe's Refugee Crisis

German Public Opinion on Refugees Is Turning

What a difference a month makes. On the night of September 4th Angela Merkel made the most dramatic decision of her decade as German chancellor: to suspend European asylum rules and allow tens of thousands of refugees stranded in Hungary to enter Germany via Austria. [...]

The numbers are dramatic. More than 200,000 migrants are believed to have arrived in Germany in September alone.
5 For the year, official forecasts had already risen in August from 450,000 to 800,000. This week *Bild*, Germany's largest tabloid, cited estimates that the number could reach 1.5m – equivalent to the population of Munich. New refugees keep pouring in, and those granted asylum have the right to bring family later. No end is in sight. [...]

Fights have broken out inside overcrowded asylum centres, often between young men of different ethnic or religious groups. There have been more arson attacks on migrant centres. In Dresden, a xenophobic movement called Pegida is
10 growing again: about 9,000 protested this Monday against refugees. [...]

The fiercest criticism of Mrs Merkel comes from within her own conservative bloc – the Christian Democratic Union (CDU), which she leads, and the Christian Social Union (CSU), which exists only in Bavaria and usually supports her. Horst Seehofer, the CSU's boss and premier of Bavaria, called Mrs Merkel's decision "a mistake that will keep us occupied for a long time". [...]
15 In response Mrs Merkel's government is scrambling to make changes. [...] More police and administrators are being hired. All Balkan countries have been declared "safe" so that their asylum applicants can be rejected and deported faster. [...]

None of this, however, will reduce the numbers of Syrians, Iraqis and Afghans who are fleeing war. Nor will last month's agreement by the European Union to allocate 120,000 refugees among member states. [...] Germans worry
20 whether Muslim refugees will accept German norms of sexual equality, secularism and Germany's special responsibility towards Israel and Jews.

[...] Mrs Merkel is under pressure as never before. Yet the crisis has brought out a new style of leadership in her. For years she has been accused of following public opinion rather than guiding it. Now she has found her moral calling. "If we start having to apologise for showing a friendly face in emergencies," she says defiantly, "then this is not my
25 country."

(364 words)

The Economist, 10 October 2015

"Blick von außen" by Gerhard Haderer, published in the German magazine *Stern*

Your task ⟫

Read the given article. Sum up the content and point out the aspects related to globalisation.

Then analyse the cartoon and compare it with the article.

3a Global Trade, Modern Slavery and Migration

PART 2: Dialogue – Topic: Working Conditions in Developing Countries

Role Card No. 2

Topic: Working Conditions in Developing Countries

Situation:

After another severe fire in a garment factory in Pakistan a panel of experts discusses ways to improve the working conditions.

Your task:

You act now as the person below. Introduce yourself to the other persons you meet in the show.

Your role:

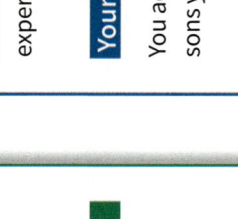

Name:	Bill Ackerman
From:	London
Age:	51
Profession:	Oxfam activist
Attitude:	Fights for human rights: workers should be better paid; working conditions should be humane.

Role Card No. 1

Topic: Working Conditions in Developing Countries

Situation:

After another severe fire in a garment factory in Pakistan a panel of experts discusses ways to improve the working conditions.

Your task:

You act now as the person below. Introduce yourself to the other persons you meet in the show.

Your role:

Name:	Saleena Zada
From:	Islamabad, Pakistan
Age:	43
Profession:	chief executive of garment factory
Attitude:	The workers should be happy to have a job; we are constantly improving the facilities and their situation.

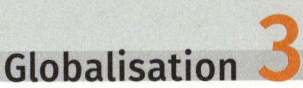
3a Global Trade, Modern Slavery and Migration

PART 2: Dialogue – Topic: Working Conditions in Developing Countries

Role Card No. 3

Topic: Working Conditions in Developing Countries

Situation:

After another severe fire in a garment factory in Pakistan a panel of experts discusses ways to improve the working conditions.

Your task:

You act now as the person below. Introduce yourself to the other persons you meet in the show.

Your role:

Name:	Shamana Singh
From:	Islamabad, Pakistan
Age:	24
Profession:	worker in a garment factory
Attitude:	Tries to organise a trade union against her employer's will; went on strike after the fire.

3b Going Hot and Cold – Environment vs. Resources ■ Team 1

PART 1: Presentation on the Effects Caused by Global Warming

Paul Braun
Global Warming Kills 150,000 a Year

At least 150,000 people die needlessly each year as a direct result of global warming, three major UN organisations warned yesterday. The belief that the effects of climate change would become apparent in 10, 20 or 50 years time was misplaced, they said in a report. The changes had already brought about a noticeable increase in malnutrition[1], as well as outbreaks of diarrhoea and malaria, the three "big killers" in the poorest countries of the world. [...] Although
5 the rises in death and diseases were most marked in poorest states, they were worldwide. Global warming led to drought[2] and a shorter growing season, and malnutrition weakened people, particularly children, making them susceptible[3] to killer diseases.

The most recent example of people being caught unawares[4] was the summer heat wave in Europe, where the initial estimates of excess deaths are still being revised upwards, with 25,482 people now known to have died in the unusu-
10 ally high temperatures, 2,045 of them in England and Wales. In some badly affected countries, such as Germany, the results have still not been made public. But beside the deaths, there was a large increase in other illnesses. Many children were admitted to hospital in England with kidney problems due to[5] dehydration. Parents and children had failed to realise that they needed to drink more to survive the heat. [...]

The report, produced by the WHO, the UN Environment Programme and the World Meteorological Programme, de-
15 tails how the increased warmth has intensified the spread of diseases. Diarrhoeal diseases[6] spread by bacteria, mostly via unclean water and food, spread and develop more quickly in warmer temperatures and humidity. [...]

Diseases spread by rats and insects are also more common in warmer weather. Malaria, dengue fever and Lyme disease[7] are all on the increase. Many threats can be curtailed[8] by dispensing[9] preventive medicine and providing clean water and sanitation. Climate change makes these issues more urgent, the report said. [...]
20 Heat stroke[10] kills the old and vulnerable; 25,842 more people than usual died in August in Europe. In the UK, a 12% increase in salmonella food poisoning is reported to health authorities for every 1 °C rise in temperature. [...]
(342 words)

The Guardian, 12 December 2003

---

[1] **malnutrition** *Unterernährung* – [2] **drought** *Dürre* – [3] **susceptible** very likely to be affected – [4] **to catch sb. unawares** *jemanden überraschen* – [5] **due to** because of – [6] **diarrhoeal diseases** *Durchfallerkrankungen* – [7] **Lyme disease** *Borreliose* – [8] **curtailed** limited – [9] **to dispense** *verteilen* – [10] **heat stroke** *Hitzschlag*

Photo published by Alaska-Tom

Your task »»

Read the given article. Sum up the content and point out the aspects related to globalisation.

Then analyse the visual and compare it with the article.

3b Going Hot and Cold – Environment vs. Resources ■ Team 2

PART 1: Presentation on Difficult Negotiations at Climate Summit

Nikhil Kumar
India's Needs for Coal-Fueled Growth Complicates Paris Climate Summit

[...] As world leaders gathered in Paris for the opening of the international climate conference on Nov. 30, excavators in a densely forested corner of eastern India were at work extracting coal at what in coming years is projected to become the biggest mine in Asia. [...]

For India's leaders, the expansion in coal generation is needed to power India's growth and lift hundreds of millions
5 of Indians out of poverty. One in five of India's 1.3 billion people continue to live without access to electricity, according to the International Energy Agency. [...]

To help with the fight against climate change, India is planning, alongside its coal push, a significant expansion in the use of renewable energy sources such as solar power. [...]

To do so, India aims to add as much as 175 gigawatts in energy generation from renewable sources by 2022. [...]

10 But even if everything goes to plan, that still means India – currently the world's third-large emitter by total – will see its carbon emissions continue climbing in coming years. This presents a challenge for delegates in Paris as they try and forge a consensus for an agreement to keep temperatures from rising more than 2 degrees Celsius (around 3.6 degrees Fahrenheit) above the levels in pre-industrial times.

From India's point of view, the burden should fall on the countries responsible for global warming, not developing
15 nations that are only beginning to grow. Historically, India accounts for only 3 % of energy-related carbon dioxide emissions since 1890, according to IEA figures. In per capita terms, India's emissions stood at 1.6 metric tons in 2014— roughly 10% of the level for the U.S. and a quarter of the level for China. [...]

India is also calling for greater support from developed countries like the U.S. to help developing nations slow emissions and adapt to climate change [...]. "India is doing as much as it can with its own resources," India's spokesman
20 at the conference, Ajay Mathur, said. "With climate financing from the developed world, we can do so much more, much faster."

(333 words)

TIME, 1 December 2015

Photo published by Getty Images on 01/06/2014

> **Your task** ⟫⟫
>
> Read the given article. Sum up the content and point out the aspects related to globalisation.
>
> Then analyse the photo and compare it with the article.

3b Going Hot and Cold – Environment vs. Resources ■ Team 3

PART 1: Presentation on the Consequences of Rising Temperatures

Michael Meacher
End of the World Nigh – It's Official

There is a lot wrong with our world. But it is not as bad as many people think. It is worse. Global warming is slowly but relentlessly changing the face of the planet.

We are only in the early stages of this process, but already carbon dioxide in the atmosphere has reached 375 parts per million, the highest level for at least half a million years. Temperatures are projected to rise by up to 5.8 C this cen-
5 tury, 10 times the increase of 0.6 C in the last century. [...] This means temperatures could rise by up to 8.1 C in some parts of the world.

[...] In China severe floods used to occur once every 20 years; now they occur in nine out of every 10. The number of people affected by floods globally has risen from 7 million in the 1960s to 150 million now. In 1998 two-thirds of Bangladesh was under water for months, affecting 30 million people. [...]

10 Flooding is only the beginning. The number of people worldwide devastated by hurricanes or cyclones has increased eightfold to 25 million a year over the past 30 years. The oceans are steadily warming, and since they currently absorb 50 times more CO_2 than is contained in the atmosphere, even a tiny reduction in CO_2 absorption by the sea could cause global temperatures to rise significantly.

Even more seriously, 10,000 billion tonnes of methane (a greenhouse gas 20 times more potent than CO_2) are stored
15 [...] on the shallow floor of the Arctic, in sediments below the seabed. If the temperature – surrounding the methane – warms, it becomes unstable and methane gas is released, causing temperatures to increase further. Warming oceans also cause the waters to expand and the sea level to rise. Sea level is predicted to rise by 3ft over the next century, leading to huge areas of Bangladesh, Egypt and China being inundated.

(314 words)

The Guardian, 14 February 2003

Greenland Tour, Climate Change 2005.
Photo published by Greenpeace/Steve Morgan

Your task ⟫⟫

Read the given article. Sum up the content and point out the aspects related to globalisation.

Then analyse the visual and compare it with the article.

3b Going Hot and Cold – Environment vs. Resources

PART 2: Dialogue – Topic: Climate Change

Role Card No. 2

Topic: Climate Change

Situation:
One year after the Paris Summit, experts discuss the reduction of CO_2 emissions and their effects.

Your task:
You act now as the person below. Introduce yourself to the other persons you meet in the discussion.

Your role:

Name:	Andrew Ross
From:	Phoenix, USA
Age:	63
Profession:	priest and preacher
Attitude:	There have always been cold and hot periods in the history of the world climate; natural phenomena like meteorites killed thousands of species; everything is God-given.

Role Card No. 1

Topic: Climate Change

Situation:
One year after the Paris Summit, experts discuss the reduction of CO_2 emissions and their effects.

Your task:
You act now as the person below. Introduce yourself to the other persons you meet in the discussion.

Your role:

Name:	Lian Yan
From:	Beijing, China
Age:	55
Profession:	politician
Attitude:	US and Europe have polluted the world for 150 years; we should have the same opportunity of development and be given the right to postpone our reduction of green house gases.

3b Going Hot and Cold – Environment vs. Resources

PART 2: Dialogue – Topic: Climate Change

Role Card No. 3

Topic: Climate Change

Situation:

One year after the Paris Summit, experts discuss the reduction of CO_2 emissions and its results.

Your task:

You act now as the person below. Introduce yourself to the other persons you meet in the discussion.

Your role:

Name:	Hedda Hansen
From:	Oslo, Norway
Age:	28
Profession:	Greenpeace activist
Attitude:	If we don't change our behaviour and attitude drastically now, our children will grow up in a disaster: wild animals will be extinct; flooding will be a major and unpredictable problem; our lives will be in danger.

3c Terrorism and Migration in the Wake of Globalisation ■ Team 1

PART 1: Presentation on the Vain Efforts of Refugees to Reach Britain

Naina Bajekal
After Paris, Life for Refugees in France Has Gotten Even Harder

It had been one of the warmest Novembers on Record, and for a while, the estimated 6,000 migrants and refugees in the French port city of Calais almost counted themselves lucky. That luck didn't last: by the middle of the month, winter was on its way, bringing the lashing rains and icy chill that everyone had feared. But the people living in the Jungle, as the camps on the outskirts of Calais are known, are bracing for more than just winter. After terrorists con-
5 nected to ISIS set off suicide bombs and gunned down Parisians in the heart of the French capital on Nov. 13, the migrants here knew they might face a tide of anti-refugee sentiment – especially when a passport registered to a Syrian migrant was found among the attackers.

The aftershocks of Paris are already being felt in Calais, where migrants – rarely welcomed to begin with – worry they are being seen as a security threat. "Some people throw glass bottles at us when we walk to the tunnel," says
10 Mima, a journalist and university graduate from Ethiopia. He spends his days helping in the camp's large Ethiopian Orthodox church known as St. Michael's, and his nights making the 14-km journey to the entrance of the Channel Tunnel, the undersea rail link connecting the U.K. to France. "I don't really blame them," he says with a shrug. "They don't want us to be here, but we don't want to be here either."

Like most of the migrants in Calais, Mima is still reluctant to accept the squalid Jungle as his home. He spent a long,
15 grueling journey dreaming of a better life in the U.K., traveling more than 4,800 km, only to wind up here in Calais, just 34 km from England's white cliffs of Dover. To cross this last distance is no easy feat. Since June, at least 19 people have died attempting to cross into England via the Channel Tunnel. They have fallen from freight trains, been hit by cars and trucks and even been electrocuted on the railway tracks. Yet they keep coming.

(340 words)

Time Magazine, 14 December 2015

Published by Reuters on 08/08/2015

Your task 》》》

Read the given article. Sum up the content and point out the aspects related to globalisation.

Then analyse the photo and compare it with the article.

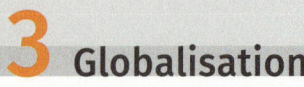

© Schöningh Verlag, Best.-Nr. 040159-3

3c Terrorism and Migration in the Wake of Globalisation ■ Team 2

PART 1: Presentation on the Reaction of Politicians to the Terror Attack in Paris

Maya Rhodan
President Obama and François Hollande Met at the White House in Wake of Terror Attack in Paris

President Obama said that the United States will stand with France to destroy the Islamic State of Iraq and Syria after the Paris attacks.

In a meeting at the White House with French President François Hollande, Obama said that ISIS "cannot be tolerated, it must be destroyed and we must do it together." "We've never forgotten how the French people stood with us after
5 9/11, and today we stand by you," he said. [...]

The meeting between the two leaders came amid a push by France to get more world leaders on board with intensified strikes against ISIS in Syria. Later this week, Hollande will meet with leaders from Italy, Germany, and Russia to talk strategy. On Monday, Hollande met with British Prime Minister David Cameron, who said he would reach out to parliament for support on increasing attacks.

10 Despite Obama's show of support, the White House has kept Hollande's request for more support for a military intervention in Syria at arm's length. Instead, Obama urged the European Union to allow airlines to share passenger information. He and Hollande also agreed to share more intelligence on terrorist threats and focus on hurting the financing and leadership of ISIS.

"It is France that came under attack on the 13th of November," Hollande said. "But by targeting France, the terrorists
15 were targeting the world."

Obama also spoke directly to the American people about the recent controversy over accepting Syrian refugees, arguing that no one goes through more screening.

"On the Statue of Liberty, a gift from the people of France ... there are words we know so well," Obama said. "That's the spirit that makes us American. That's the spirit that binds the U.S. to France. That's the spirit we need today."

20 Asked by a reporter about the Turkish downing of a Russian fighter jet, Obama said that his top priority was making sure that it did not escalate, arguing that Russia should work more closely on counterterrorism efforts.

"What took place means that we must find a solution to the Syrian crisis," Hollande added. "We know what the stakes are when we don't do that."

(352 words)

Time Magazine, 24 November 2015

Advertisement published in a magazine
in China in 2005

Your task >>>

> Read the given article.
> Sum up the content and
> point out the aspects
> related to globalisation.
>
> Then analyse the visual
> and compare it with the
> article.

3c Terrorism and Migration in the Wake of Globalisation ■ Team 3

PART 1: Presentation on the Future of Our Children in a Globalised World

Jared Diamond
Lessons from Lost Worlds

Children have a wonderful ability to focus their parents' attention on the essentials. Before our twin sons were born in 1987, I had often heard about all the environmental problems projected to come to a head toward the middle of this century. But I was born in 1937, so I would surely be dead before 2050. [...]

After the birth of our kids [...] I realized with a jolt: my kids will reach my present age of 65 in 2052. [...]

5 Over the heads of our own children now hang other threats from world conditions, different from the threats of 1939 – 45.

While the risk of nuclear war between major powers still exists, it's less acute than 15 years ago, thank God. Many people worry about terrorists, and so do I, but then I reflect that terrorists could at worst kill "only" a few tens of millions of us. The even graver problems that could do in all our children are environmental ones, such as global warm-

10 ing and land and water degradation.

These threats interact with terrorism by breeding the desperation that drives some individuals to become terrorists and others to support terrorists. Sept. 11 made us realize that we are not immune from the environmental problems of any country, no matter how remote – not even those of Somalia and Afghanistan. Of course, in reality, that was true before Sept. 11, but we didn't think much about it then. We and the Somalis breathe and pollute the same atmosphere,

15 are bathed by the same oceans and compete for the same global pie of shrinking resources. Before Sept. 11, though, we thought of globalization as mainly meaning "us" sending "them" good things, like the Internet and Coca-Cola. Now we understand that globalization also means "them" being in a position to send "us" bad things, like terrorist attacks, emerging diseases, illegal immigrants and situations requiring the dispatch of U.S. troops. [...]

We face big problems that will do us in if we don't solve them. But we are capable of solving them. The risk we face

20 isn't that of an asteroid collision beyond our ability to avoid. Instead our problems are of our own making, and so we can stop making them. The only thing lacking is the necessary political will.

(350 words)

Time Magazine, 2 September 2002

Scene from *The Day After Tomorrow*, 2004

Your task 》》

Read the given article. Sum up the content and point out the aspects related to globalisation.

Then analyse the film still and compare it with the article.

3c Terrorism and Migration in the Wake of Globalisation

PART 2: Dialogue – Topic: Refugees

Role Card No. 2

Topic: Refugees

Situation:

You take part in a discussion on TV after thousands of refugees succeeded in fleeing through the Channel Tunnel to Dover. Should they be sent back?

Your task:

You act now as the person below. Introduce yourself to the other persons you meet in the show.

Your role:

Name:	David Cameron
From:	London
Age:	50
Profession:	Politician
Attitude:	We were forced to cope with too many immigrants in the past, so that we have to think of new restrictions on immigrant influx.

Role Card No. 1

Topic: Refugees

Situation:

You take part in a discussion on TV after thousands of refugees succeeded in fleeing through the Channel Tunnel to Dover. Should they be sent back?

Your task:

You act now as the person below. Introduce yourself to the other persons you meet in the show.

Your role:

Name:	Abdul Omar
From:	Aleppo, Syria
Age:	27
Profession:	refugee
Attitude:	After bombs had destroyed our house in Aleppo, we first went to a refugee camp in Lebanon, but the conditions there were so terrible that I had to bring my family to Europe. My brother has lived in London for five years.

3c Terrorism and Migration in the Wake of Globalisation

PART 2: Dialogue – Topic: Refugees

Role Card No. 3

Topic: Refugees

Situation:

You take part in a discussion on TV after thousands of refugees succeeded in fleeing through the Channel Tunnel to Dover. Should they be sent back?

Your task:

You act now as the person below. Introduce yourself to the other persons you meet in the show.

Your role:

Name:	Professor Alexia Thomas
From:	London
Age:	63
Profession:	human rights activist
Attitude:	She shares the experiences of the refugees and knows how it feels not to be welcomed; Britain needs refugees for economic reasons; Britain has been a multi-cultural society for a long time now.

4a Utopia & Dystopia ■ Team 1

PART 1: Presentation on the Horrors of the Future

Margaret Atwood
The Handmaid's Tale

This is the one good thing about these evenings, the evenings of the Ceremony: I'm allowed to watch the news. It seems to be an unspoken rule in this household: we always get here on time, he's always late, Serena always lets us watch the news.

Such as it is: who knows if any of it is true? It could be old clips, it could be faked. But I watch it anyway, hoping to be
5   able to read beneath it. Any news, now, is better than none.

First, the front lines. They are not lines, really: the war seems to be going on in many places at once.

Wooded hills, seen from above, the trees a sickly yellow. I wish she'd fix the color. The Appalachian Highlands, says the voice-over, where the Angels of the Apocalypse, Fourth Division, are smoking out a pocket[1] of Baptist guerillas, with air support from the Twenty-first Battalion of the Angels of Light. We are shown two helicopters, black ones
10   with silver wings painted on the sides. Below them, a clump[2] of trees explodes.

Now a close shot of a prisoner, with a stubbled and dirty face, flanked by two Angels in their neat black uniforms. […] They show us only victories, never defeats. Who wants bad news?

Possibly he's an actor.

The anchorman[3] comes on now. His manner is kindly, fatherly; he gazes out at us from the screen, looking, with his
15   tan and his white hair and candid eyes, wise wrinkles around them, like everybody's ideal grandfather. What he's telling us, his level smile implies, is for our own good. Everything will be all right soon. I promise. There will be peace. You must trust. You must go to sleep, like good children.

He tells us what we long to believe. He's very convincing.

I struggle against him. He's like an old movie star, I tell myself, with false teeth and a face job. At the same time I sway
20   towards him, like one hypnotized. If only it were true. If only I could believe.

(341 words)

Margaret Atwood: *The Handmaid's Tale*. Vintage, London 1996, pp. 92 f.

_____

[1] **pocket** *Widerstandsnest* – [2] **clump of trees** *Baumgruppe* – [3] **anchorman** *Nachrichtenmoderator*

4a Utopia & Dystopia ■ Team 1

PART 1: Presentation on the Horrors of the Future

The film still is taken from the 1990 adaptation of the novel *The Handmaid's Tale*. An execution of a man who harassed and abused a woman is prepared. The handmaids (are supposed to) shout their insults at the man before they kick him, pull out his hair and finally stone him to death.

Your task ⟫⟫

> Read the given excerpt. Sum up the content and point out whether the text is from a dystopian or a utopian novel.
>
> Then analyse the film still and relate it to the excerpt.

4a Utopia & Dystopia ■ Team 2

PART 1: Presentation on the Horrors of the Future

H.G. Wells
The Time Machine

The enemy I dreaded[1] may surprise you. It was the darkness of the new moon. [...] Each night there was a longer interval of darkness. And I now understood to some slight degree at least the reason of the fear of the little Upper-world people[2] for the dark. I wondered vaguely what foul villany[3] it might be that the Morlocks did under the new moon. I felt pretty sure now that my second hypothesis was all wrong. The Upper-world people might once have
5 been the favoured aristocracy, and the Morlocks their mechanical servants: but that had long since passed away. The two species that had resulted from the evolution of man were sliding down towards, or had already arrived at, an altogether new relationship. The Eloi, like the Carolingian kings, had decayed to a mere beautiful futility[4]. They still possessed the earth on sufferance[5]: since the Morlocks, subterranean for innumerable generations, had come at last to find the daylit surface intolerable. And the Morlocks made their garments[6], I inferred, and maintained them in their
10 habitual needs, perhaps through the survival of an old habit of service. They did it as a standing horse paws with his foot, or as a man enjoys killing animals in sport: because ancient and departed necessities had impressed it on the organism. But, clearly, the old order was already in part reversed. The Nemesis[7] of the delicate ones was creeping on apace[8]. Ages ago, thousands of generations ago, man had thrust his brother man out of the ease and the sunshine. And now that brother was coming back changed! Already the Eloi had begun to learn one old lesson anew. They were
15 becoming reacquainted with Fear. And suddenly there came into my head the memory of the meat I had seen in the Under-world. It seemed odd how it floated into my mind: not stirred up as it were by the current of my meditations, but coming in almost like a question from outside. I tried to recall the form of it. I had a vague sense of something familiar, but I could not tell what it was at the time.

(355 words)

H.G. Wells: *The Time Machine*. Penguin, Harmondsworth 1927, Chapter VII, pp. 54 f.

---

[1] **to dread** to fear – [2] **the little Upper-world people** the Eloi: *auf der Erde leben zwei Spezies, die kindlichen Eloi über der Erdoberfläche, die affenähnlich aussehenden Morlocks unter der Erdoberfläche* – [3] **villany** *Schurkerei* – [4] **futility** *Sinn und Zwecklosigkeit* – [5] **on sufferance** *unter stillschweigender Duldung* – [6] **garments** clothes – [7] **Nemesis** *der Untergang, die gerechte Strafe* – [8] **apace** quickly

4a Utopia & Dystopia ■ Team 2

PART 1: Presentation on the Horrors of the Future

The film still is taken from the 2014 movie *The Giver*. In this movie a so-called perfect world is presented, where everything is controlled by strict rules. The "perfect world" is completely isolated from "Elsewhere", every other place in the world. No evidence of disease, hunger, poverty, war, or lasting pain exists in the community. The picture shows Jonas' family during a ceremony, in which he – like all other youths of a given age – is presented his future task in the perfect society. Jonas is meant to be "the Receiver" who is introduced to all relevant memories of the past which are not shared by other members of the society.

Your task 》》》

> Read the given excerpt. Sum up the content and point out whether the text is from a dystopian or a utopian novel.
>
> Then analyse the film still and relate it to the excerpt.

4a Utopia & Dystopia ■ Team 2

PART 1: Presentation on the Horrors of the Future

4a Utopia & Dystopia ■ Team 3

PART 1: Presentation on the Horrors of the Future

Matt Haig
Echo Boy

The thing burning into my shoulder caused me a significant amount of pain.

My arms were strapped tight. I was in some kind of a container. My body was in thick liquid up to my neck.

The liquid was rising slowly. It was now touching my chin.

At first this was a passive observation, and one made without knowing such words as "liquid" and "chin".

5 But slowly there came an instinct. [...] Panic.

Without understanding why, I felt I had to get out of there. I pulled desperately on the straps. I screamed. The scream was not a word. [...] The scream was just noise. A desperate roar that gave me enough strength for my arms, then legs, to break free of their constraints[1].

This is when I started banging on the side of the tank.

10 I kept banging and screaming until I heard something that wasn't a bang or a scream. [...] A noise. Something getting nearer. Someone.

It was a woman. I know that now, but I didn't know it then. [...] She had something in her hand. It was small and grey and moving. If I'd ever seen a centipede[2], I might have thought it was one. Though, of course, it wasn't. It wasn't anything alive. She placed it between her thumb and her finger and mimed putting it in her ear, and then pointed it at me.

15 At my ear.

I understood enough about this instruction to put it to my ear after she had given it to me. Within seconds it was moving in my head. I could feel it inside me. It wasn't painful. It wasn't even weird, because to find something weird you have to have had experience of normality. But I didn't have experience of anything.

Then I must have shut down. That thing inside my head had shut me down. Because there was a gap. A time that I
20 can't remember. A gap during which I was born.

When I woke up, everything was different. I understood things.

(324 words)

Matt Haig: *Echo Boy*. Random House, London 2015, Chapter 1, pp. 137 ff.

---

[1] **constraints** sth. that limits your freedom – [2] **centipede** a small worm-like animal with a lot of legs, *Tausendfüßer*

4a Utopia & Dystopia ■ Team 3

PART 1: Presentation on the Horrors of the Future

Below: a film still taken from the 1999 movie *The Matrix*. The still shows Neo's rebirth, whereas Matt Haig's protagonist Daniel (*Echo Boy*) does a mind-log, a sort of future diary for recording your thoughts, about his birth. In *Echo Boy*, the future is dominated by big corporations. Global warming has left half the world scorched (= *verbrannt, versengt*), half drowned. The police and politicians are dominated by the oligarchs. The rich reside in mansions protected by robot dogs, whereas the poor live in slums. Much of the manual work and most domestic labour is performed by humanoid robots, the latest generation of which are called Echos (Enhanced Computerised Humanoid Organisms) – physically perfect but without emotions.

Your task »»

Read the given excerpt. Sum up the content and point out whether the text is from a dystopian or a utopian novel.

Then analyse the film still and relate it to the excerpt.

4a Utopia & Dystopia

PART 2: Dialogue – Topic: Food Engineering

Role Card No. 2

Topic: Food Engineering

Situation:

The EU has finally agreed upon permitting the consumption of genetically-modified food in its member countries. After a huge demonstration against this decision you take part in a panel discussion broadcast on TV.

Your task:

You act now as the person below. Introduce yourself to the other persons you meet in the show.

Your role:

Name:	Liv Thore
From:	Oslo, Norway
Age:	31
Profession:	Greenpeace activist
Attitude:	As an environmentalist and mother of three children she is concerned about the long-term consequences of consuming genetically-modified food, in particular since there are no studies about its influence on people's health.

Role Card No. 1

Topic: Food Engineering

Situation:

The EU has finally agreed upon permitting the consumption of genetically-modified food in its member countries. After a huge demonstration against this decision you take part in a panel discussion broadcast on TV.

Your task:

You act now as the person below. Introduce yourself to the other persons you meet in the show.

Your role:

Name:	Kerry J. Preete
From:	Saskatchewan, Canada
Age:	49
Profession:	Executive Vice President, Global Strategy, Monsanto
Attitude:	Against the background of a massive global increase in population, agriculture will need to become more productive and more sustainable; we are committed to developing technologies that enable farmers to produce more crops by also modifying them genetically.

4a Utopia & Dystopia

PART 2: Dialogue – Topic: Food Engineering

Role Card No. 3

Topic: Food Engineering

Situation:

The EU has finally agreed upon admitting the comsumption of genetically-modified food in its member countries. After a huge demonstration against this decision you take part in a panel discussion broadcast on TV.

Your task:

You act now as the person below. Introduce yourself to the other persons you meet in the show.

Your role:

Name:	Bernadette Dunham
From:	Washington, D.C.
Age:	53
Profession:	Ph. D., Director, Center for Veterinary Medicine
Attitude:	She sees opportunities in genetically-modified food in the fight against hunger, in coping with climate change and creating new jobs. However, she is aware of the fact that tight controls must be implemented.

4b Utopia & Dystopia ■ Team 1

PART 1: Presentation on the Horrors of the Future

Margaret Atwood
The Handmaid's Tale

It was after the catastrophe, when they shot the President and machine-gunned the Congress and the army declared a state of emergency. They blamed it on the Islamic fanatics, at the time.

Keep calm, they said on television. Everything is under control.

I was stunned. Everyone was, I know that. It was hard to believe. The entire government, gone like that. How did they
5 get in, how did it happen?

That was when they suspended[1] the Constitution. They said it would be temporary. There wasn't even any rioting in the streets. People stayed home at night, watching television, looking for some direction. There wasn't even an enemy you could put your finger on.

Look out, said Moira to me, over the phone. Here it comes.

10 Here comes what? I said.

You wait, she said. They've been building up to this. It's you and me up against the wall, baby. She was quoting an expression of my mother's, but she wasn't intending to be funny.

Things continued in that state of suspended animation for weeks, although some things did happen. Newspapers were censored and some were closed down, for security reasons they said. The roadblocks began to appear, and Iden-
15 tipasses[2].

Everyone approved of that, since it was obvious you couldn't be too careful. They said that new elections would be held, but that it would take some time to prepare for them. The thing to do, they said, was to continue on as usual. [...]

The next morning, on my way to the library for the day, I stopped by the same store for another pack, because I'd run out. I was smoking more those days, it was the tension, you could feel it, like a subterranean hum[3], although things
20 seemed so quiet. I was drinking more coffee too, and having trouble sleeping. Everyone was a little jumpy[4]. There was a lot more music on the radio than usual, and fewer words.

(350 words)

Margaret Atwood: *The Handmaid's Tale*. Vintage, London 1996, pp. 182 f.

---

[1] **to suspend** to annul – [2] **Identipasses** special IDs – [3] **hum** *Brummen* – [4] **jumpy** nervous

4b Utopia & Dystopia ■ Team 1

PART 1: Presentation on the Horrors of the Future

The film still is taken from the 1990 adaptation of the novel *The Handmaid's Tale*. Everyone dresses alike within their own social group, thus a social ranking becomes obvious. Women are divided into a small range of social categories, each one signified by a specifically coloured dress in a similar style. Handmaids (servants) wear red. The dress code means that women are no longer individuals; they have become interchangeable.

Your task 》》》

> Read the given excerpt. Sum up the content and point out whether the text is from a dystopian or a utopian novel.
>
> Then analyse the film still and relate it to the excerpt.

4b Utopia & Dystopia ■ Team 1

PART 1: Presentation on the Horrors of the Future

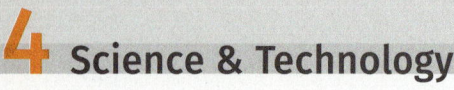

4b Utopia & Dystopia ▪ Team 2

PART 1: Presentation on the Horrors of the Future

George Orwell
Nineteen Eighty-Four

"Up with your hands!" yelled a savage voice.

A handsome, tough-looking boy of nine had popped up from behind the table and was menacing[1] him with a toy automatic pistol, while his small sister, about two years younger, made the same gesture with a fragment of wood. Both of them were dressed in the blue shorts, grey shirts, and red neckerchiefs[2] which were the uniform of the Spies. Win-
5 ston raised his hands above his head, but with an uneasy feeling, so vicious[3] was the boy's demeanour[4], that it was not altogether a game.

"You're a traitor[5]!" yelled the boy. "You're a thought-criminal! You're a Eurasian[6] spy! I'll shoot you, I'll vaporize[7] you, I'll send you to the salt mines!"

Suddenly they were both leaping round him, shouting "Traitor!" and "Thought-criminal!" the little girl imitating her
10 brother in every movement. It was somehow slightly frightening, like the gambolling[8] of tiger cubs[9] which will soon grow up into man-eaters. There was a sort of calculating ferocity[10] in the boy's eye, a quite evident desire to hit or kick Winston and a consciousness of being very nearly big enough to do so. It was a good job it was not a real pistol he was holding, Winston thought.

Mrs Parsons' eyes flitted nervously from Winston to the children, and back again. In the better light of the living-
15 room. […]

"They do get so noisy," she said. "They're disappointed because they couldn't go to see the hanging, that's what it is. I'm too busy to take them and Tom won't be back from work in time."

"Why can't we go and see the hanging?" roared the boy in his huge voice.

"Want to see the hanging! Want to see the hanging!" chanted the little girl, still capering[11] round.
20 Some Eurasian prisoners, guilty of war crimes, were to be hanged in the Park that evening, Winston remembered. This happened about once a month, and was a popular spectacle. Children always clamoured[12] to be taken to see it.

(331 words)

George Orwell: *Nineteen Eighty-Four*. Penguin, Harmondsworth 1954, Chapter 1, pp. 22 f.

––––––––––

[1] **menacing** threatening – [2] **neckerchief** cloth or scarf worn round the neck – [3] **vicious** done with evil intent – [4] **demeanour** way of behaving – [5] **traitor** *Verräter* – [6] **Eurasian** belonging to Eurasia, one of the three fictitious superpowers in Orwell's novel – [7] **to vaporize** to reduce a substance to gaseous form by heat – [8] **to gambol** *herumtollen, herumspringen* – [9] **tiger cub** *Tigerbaby* – [10] **ferocity** *Grausamkeit* – [11] **to caper** *herumhüpfen* – [12] **to clamour** to demand loudly

4b Utopia & Dystopia ■ Team 2

PART 1: Presentation on the Horrors of the Future

The film still is taken from the 2007 adaptation of the novel *Nineteen Eighty-Four*. Orwell portrays a state in which the government monitors and controls every aspect of human life by means of telescreens and hidden microphones across the city. Big Brother is the face of the Party. The citizens are told that he is the leader of the nation and the head of the Party. "INGSOC" is an acronym for "English Socialism," the political philosophy of the Party.

The telescreens also monitor human behaviour and even having a disloyal thought is against the law. Everywhere citizens are continuously reminded by the omnipresent signs reading "BIG BROTHER IS WATCHING YOU," that the authorities are scrutinizing (= *genau untersuchen*) them. In addition, the Party undermines family structure by inducting children into an organization called the *Junior Spies*, which brainwashes and encourages them to spy on their parents and report any instance of disloyalty to the Party.

Your task »»

Read the given excerpt. Sum up the content and point out whether the text is from a dystopian or a utopian novel.

Then analyse the film still and relate it to the excerpt.

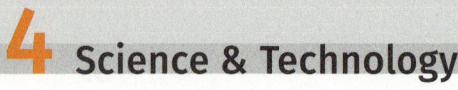

4b Utopia & Dystopia ■ Team 3

PART 1: Presentation on the Horrors of the Future

Ben Peek
Black Sheep

I was convicted of being Japanese. It was my only crime, and when found guilty, I was sentenced to Assimilation.[1] […]
Inside Sol Demic's[2] halls, neon lights swept over my face. The walls were white, new born but sterile, and there was
no sound beyond the stumbling trip of my feet and my chains. The Segregators never said a word, never told me
when to turn into a doorway, or when to stop. They used their nightsticks: digging into my back to get me to move
5 faster, slapping my right side to have me turn right, my left to go left.
Eventually I reached a door that didn't open, and I waited for one of the Segregators to open it.
It had been one hour since my trial had finished.
The Judge, a dour[3], sagging[4], sinking past his bones old man, had said: "Isao Dazai[5], you have broken the United Nations Laws of Nationality. In doing this, you have put the good people of Asian-Sydney in danger of Multiculturalism,
10 a most heinous crime for which we, as People of the World, must be ever vigilant against. The court has viewed the
evidence that has been presented before us, and we find that not only are you Japanese, but that you are Japanese
with full awareness that you are living in Australia. Your willing embrace of this state, your flaunting[6] of it actually, is
nothing less than frightening, and we are forced to worry just what impact you have had on those around you. I am
forced to ask myself just how scared your family are, and find myself with no alternative than to recommend coun-
15 seling for them, while for you, Isao Dazai, I have only one choice. It is the ruling of this court that your punishment
be the only kind that can be given to someone of your … illness. We find that you will be Assimilated."
No one had said a word to me afterward.
(327 words)

Ben Peek: *Black Sheep*. Prime Books, Germantown 2007, Chapter 1, pp. 9 ff.

---

[1] **assimilation** here: a radical and invasive punishment created by the Australian government stripping the individual of his personality and skin pigmentation and leaving him with nothing but a number to identify himself – [2] **Sol Demic:** Assimilation Centre – [3] **dour** *verdrießlich* – [4] **sagging** *übellaunig* – [5] **Isao Dazai** a Japanese-born man, who has recently immigrated to Australia with his family – [6] **to flaunt** *zur Schau stellen*

4b Utopia & Dystopia ■ Team 3

PART 1: Presentation on the Horrors of the Future

Black Sheep tells the story of Isao Dazai, a Japanese-born man who has recently immigrated to Australia. The future that Isao lives in is a world of mass race segregation where each of the world's cities have been divided into three separate walled ghettos. Isao knows that wanting to cross the city's boundaries is one of the greatest of crimes in this new world, as is his inability to leave his Japanese culture behind. He is charged with the crime of multiculturalism and sentenced to assimilation. This new punishment strips Isao of his personality and skin pigmentation and leaves him with cold, white skin, and nothing but a number to identify himself with.

The given drawing from a card game shows segregators using instruments for torturing and segregating subordinates.

Your task »»

> Read the given excerpt. Sum up the content and point out whether the text is from a dystopian or a utopian novel.
>
> Then analyse the drawing and relate it to the excerpt.

4b Utopia & Dystopia

PART 2: Dialogue – Topic: Surrogacy

Role Card No. 2

Topic: Surrogacy

Situation:
You take part in a BBC TV show in Britain. The topic of the discussion is "Should surrogacy be legalized in the U.K.?".

Your task:
You act now as the person below. Introduce yourself to the other persons you meet in the show.

Your role:

Name:	Richard John Carew Chartres
From:	London
Age:	69
Profession:	bishop
Attitude:	Britain has banned commercial surrogacy; government studies have concluded that the practice is ethically unacceptable. It has a great potential for psychological injury to the child, when he/she realizes that he/she was born, not out of a loving relationship, but as the outcome of a cold, usually financial arrangement.

Role Card No. 1

Topic: Surrogacy

Situation:
You take part in a BBC show in Britain. The topic of the discussion is "Should surrogacy be legalized in the U.K.?".

Your task:
You act now as the person below. Introduce yourself to the other persons you meet in the show.

Your role:

Name:	Elton John
From:	London
Age:	69
Profession:	singer, composer
Attitude:	As two gay males my partner David Furnish and I had to fulfil our dream of having a child with the help of a surrogate mother in California. We suffered from harsh criticism by opponents who denounced our approach as "baby buying" and "treating children as commodities".

4b Utopia & Dystopia

PART 2: Dialogue – Topic: Surrogacy

Role Card No. 3

Topic: Surrogacy

Situation:

You take part in a BBC TV show in Britain. The topic of the discussion is "Should surrogacy be legalized in the U.K.?".

Your task:

You act now as the person below. Introduce yourself to the other persons you meet in the show.

Your role:

Name:	Benita Thompson
From:	Manchester
Age:	34
Profession:	surrogate mother
Attitude:	Surrogacy is definitely a way to bring happiness into the life of a childless couple. I am pleased I could help these people, and I find it a fulfilling job for me.

4c Utopia & Dystopia ■ Team 1

PART 1: Presentation on the Horrors of the Future

Aldous Huxley
Brave New World

A squat[1] grey building of only thirty-four stories. Over the main entrance the words, CENTRAL LONDON HATCH-ERY[2] AND CONDITIONING CENTRE, and, in a shield, the World State's motto, COMMUNITY, IDENTITY, STABIL-ITY. [...]

"And this," said the Director opening the door, "is the Fertilizing Room."

5 Bent over their instruments, three hundred Fertilizers[3] were plunged, as the Director of Hatcheries and Conditioning entered the room, in the scarcely breathing silence, the absent-minded, soliloquizing[4] hum[5] or whistle, of absorbed concentration. A troop of newly arrived students, very young, pink and callow[6], followed nervously, rather abjectly[7], at the Director's heels. Each of them carried a notebook, in which, whenever the great man spoke, he desperately scribbled. Straight from the horse's mouth[8]. It was a rare privilege. The D.H.C. for Central London always made a

10 point of[9] personally conducting his new students round the various departments.

"Just to give you a general idea," he would explain to them. For of course some sort of general idea they must have, if they were to do their work intelligently – though as little of one, if they were to be good and happy members of soci-ety, as possible. For particulars[10], as everyone knows, make for virtue[11] and happiness; generalities are intellectually necessary evils. Not philosophers but fret-sawyers[12] and stamp collectors compose the backbone of society.

15 "Tomorrow," he would add, smiling at them with a slightly menacing[13] geniality[14], "you'll be settling down to serious work. You won't have time for generalities[15]. Meanwhile ..."

Meanwhile, it was a privilege. Straight from the horse's mouth into the notebook. The boys scribbled like mad.

Tall and rather thin but upright, the Director advanced into the room. He had a long chin and big rather prominent teeth, just covered, when he was not talking, by his full, floridly curved lips. Old, young? Thirty? Fifty? Fifty-five? It

20 was hard to say. And anyhow the question didn't arise; in this year of stability, A.F.632[16], it didn't occur to you to ask[17] it.

(331 words)

Aldous Huxley: *Brave New World.* Vintage, London 1994, Chapter 1, pp. 1 f.

---

[1] **squat** short and thick in an unattractive way, *gedrungen* – [2] **hatchery** *Brutstätte* – [3] **Fertilizer** *here:* worker whose job it is to fertilize – [4] **to solilo-quize** to speak to oneself as if alone – [5] **hum** *Summen* – [6] **callow** with very little experience – [7] **abjectly** lacking all pride or self-respect – [8] **straight from the horse's mouth** direct from the source – [9] **to make a point of doing sth.** to do sth. very deliberately, – [10] **particulars** details, practical facts – [11] **virtue** *Tugendhaftigkeit* – [12] **fret-sawyer** sb. who uses a fret-saw (*Laubsäge*), i. e. sb whose hobby is working with wood – [13] **menacing** threatening – [14] **geniality** friendliness – [15] **generalities** general ideas, abstractions – [16] **A. F.** after Ford (instead of using A. D., Anno Domini, this society uses A. F.) – [17] **it didn't occur to you to ask** you would never think of asking

4c Utopia & Dystopia ▪ Team 1

PART 1: Presentation on the Horrors of the Future

In *Brave New World* every possible aid to reproduction is employed to create the next generation of pre-determined citizens.

The artificial womb already exists. In Tokyo, researchers have developed a technique called EUFI – extrauterine fetal incubation. They have taken goat fetuses, threaded (= *durchziehen*) catheters through the large vessels (= *Gefäße*) in the umbilical cord (= *Nabelschnur*) and supplied the fetuses with oxygenated blood while suspending them in incubators that contain artificial fluid heated to body temperature.

Your task ⟫

> Read the given excerpt. Sum up the content and point out whether the text is from a dystopian or a utopian novel.
>
> Then analyse the visual and relate it to the excerpt.

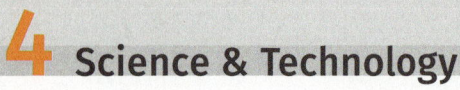

4c Utopia & Dystopia ■ Team 2

PART 1: Presentation on the Horrors of the Future

Suzanne Collins
The Hunger Games

Just as the town clock strikes two, the mayor steps up to the podium and begins to read. It's the same story every year. He tells of the history of Panem, the country that rose up out of the ashes of a place that was once called North America. He lists the disasters, the droughts[1], the storms, the fires, the encroaching[2] seas that swallowed up so much of the land, the brutal war for what little sustenance remained. The result was Panem, a shining Capitol ringed by
5 thirteen districts, which brought peace and prosperity[3] to its citizens. Then came the Dark Days, the uprising of the districts against the Capitol. Twelve were defeated, the thirteenth obliterated[4]. The Treaty of Treason gave us the new laws to guarantee peace and, as our yearly reminder that the Dark Days must never be repeated, it gave us the Hunger Games.

The rules of the Hunger Games are simple. In punishment for the uprising[5], each of the twelve districts must provide
10 one girl and one boy, called tributes, to participate. The twenty-four tributes will be imprisoned in a vast outdoor arena that could hold anything from a burning desert to a frozen wasteland. Over a period of several weeks, the competitors must fight to the death. The last tribute standing wins.

Taking the kids from our districts, forcing them to kill one another while we watch – this is the Capitol's way of reminding us how totally we are at their mercy[6]. How little chance we would stand of surviving another rebellion.
15 Whatever words they use, the real message is clear. "Look how we take your children and sacrifice them and there's nothing you can do. If you lift a finger, we will destroy every last one of you. Just as we did in District Thirteen."

To make it humiliating[7] as well as torturous[8], the Capitol requires us to treat the Hunger Games as a festivity, a sporting event pitting every district against the others.

(330 words)

Suzanne Collins: *The Hunger Games.* Part 1: "The Tributes". Scholastic Press, New York 2008, Chapter 1, pp. 18 ff.

---

[1] **drought** hard time when no rain falls at all, *Dürre* – [2] **to encroach** come nearer and bigger threateningly – [3] **prosperity** *Wohlstand* – [4] **to obliterate** to eliminate – [5] **uprising** revolution, rebellion – [6] **to be at sb.'s mercy** to depend totally on sb., to be their slave – [7] **humiliating** *demütigend, erniedrigend* – [8] **torturous** *quälend*

4c Utopia & Dystopia ▪ Team 2

PART 1: Presentation on the Horrors of the Future

The film still is taken from the 2014 adaptation of the novel *Hunger Games*. The still shows Effie, who works as the escort for District 12, and Katniss Everdeen. Katniss and her family come from District 12, a coal-mining district that is the poorest and least populated district in the autocratic nation of Panem. In the course of the first book, *The Hunger Games*, Katniss volunteers to replace her twelve-year-old sister, Primrose "Prim" Everdeen, after she has been chosen to compete in the 74th Hunger Games, a televised fight to death. When Effie asks for a round of applause for Katniss, the audience remains silent and Effie is left on stage clapping by herself in an effort to lighten the atmosphere.

Your task 》》》

Read the given excerpt. Sum up the content and point out whether the text is from a dystopian or a utopian novel.

Then analyse the film still and relate it to the excerpt.

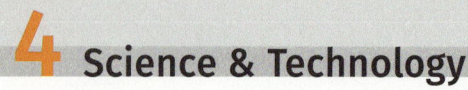

4c Utopia & Dystopia ■ Team 3

PART 1: Presentation on the Horrors of the Future

Ray Bradbury
Fahrenheit 451

It was a pleasure to burn.

It was a special pleasure to see things eaten, to see things blackened and changed. With the brass nozzle[1] in his fists, with this great python spitting its venomous[2] kerosene upon the world, the blood pounded in his head, and his hands were the hands of some amazing conductor[3] playing all the symphonies of blazing and burning to bring down the
5 tatters and charcoal ruins of history. With his symbolic helmet numbered 451 on his stolid[4] head, and his eyes all orange flame with the thought of what came next, he flicked the igniter and the house jumped up in a gorging fire that burned the evening sky red and yellow and black. He strode[5] in a swarm of fireflies. He wanted above all, like the old joke, to shove a marshmallow on a stick in the furnace, while the flapping pigeon-winged books died on the porch and lawn of the house. While the books went up in sparkling whirls and blew away on a wind turned dark with burn-
10 ing.

Montag grinned the fierce grin of all men singed[6] and driven back by flame.

He knew that when he returned to the firehouse, he might wink[7] at himself, a minstrel man[8], burnt-corked[9], in the mirror. Later, going to sleep, he would feel the fiery smile still gripped by his face muscles, in the dark. It never went away, that smile, it never ever went away, as long as he remembered.
15 He hung up his black beetle-colored helmet and shined it; he hung his flameproof jacket neatly; he showered luxuriously, and then, whistling, hands in pockets, walked across the upper floor of the fire station and fell down the hole. At the last moment, when disaster seemed positive, he pulled his hands from his pockets and broke his fall by grasping the golden pole. He slid to a squeaking halt, the heels one inch from the concrete floor downstairs.

(327 words)

Ray Bradbury: *Fahrenheit 451*. HarperCollins UK, London 2013, Chapter 1, pp. 9 f.

_____

[1] **brass nozzle** *Messingdüse* – [2] **venomous** poisonous – [3] **conductor** *Dirigent* – [4] **stolid** not showing much emotion – [5] **to stride (strode)** to walk with long steps – [6] **to singe sth.** *etwas ansengen* – [7] **to wink at sb.** *jdm. zuzwinkern* – [8] **minstrel man** *Bänkelsänger, Spielmann* – [9] **burnt-corked** *here:* black-faced

4c Utopia & Dystopia ■ Team 3

PART 1: Presentation on the Horrors of the Future

On the book cover you can see Guy Montag, the protagonist of Ray Bradbury's novel *Fahrenheit 451*, who works as a fireman. Firemen are there to detect and burn books, which are regarded as illegal, with the help of flamethrowers.

Montag at first enjoys the sensual experience of burning and does not reflect on what he is doing. Later on the protagonist more and more questions the righteousness of the state, especially after an old woman burns herself to death with her books rather than leave her library. His internal confusion makes him rethink the values of the totalitarian state he is living in.

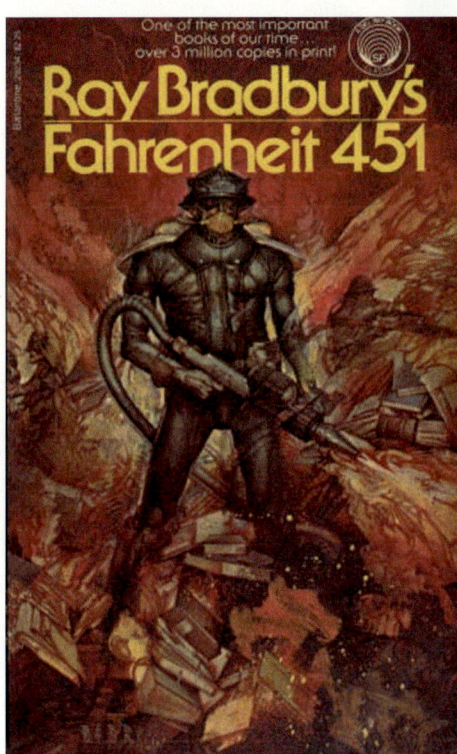

Your task 》》

Read the given excerpt. Sum up the content and point out whether the text is from a dystopian or a utopian novel.

Then analyse the book cover and relate it to the excerpt.

4c Utopia & Dystopia ■ Team 3

PART 1: Presentation on the Horrors of the Future

4c Utopia & Dystopia

PART 2: Dialogue – Topic: Designer Babies

Role Card No. 2

Topic: Designer Babies

Situation:

After a decline of natural parenthood a debate about in-vitro-fertilisation has begun. You take part in a radio discussion in California.

Your task:

You act now as the person below. Introduce yourself to the other persons you meet in the show.

Your role:

Name:	John Walker
From:	Sacramento, CA
Age:	54
Profession:	politician
Attitude:	To play God has its limits. We should not interfere with nature's process of determination. It is against all ethical principles.

Role Card No. 1

Topic: Designer Babies

Situation:

After a decline of natural parenthood a debate about in-vitro-fertilisation has begun. You take part in a radio discussion in California.

Your task:

You act now as the person below. Introduce yourself to the other persons you meet in the show.

Your role:

Name:	Marion Thunderbird
From:	San Francisco, CA
Age:	36
Profession:	scientist
Attitude:	Latest research is making designer babies a reality now, using technology developed originally for use in animals. Most parents would not hesitate to help their children to achieve their maximum potential.

4c Utopia & Dystopia

PART 2: Dialogue – Topic: Designer Babies

Role Card No. 3

Topic: Designer Babies

Situation:

After a decline of natural parenthood a debate about in-vitro-fertilisation has begun. You take part in a radio discussion in California.

Your task:

You act now as the person below. Introduce yourself to the other persons you meet in the show.

Your role:

Name:	Robert Steffenson
From:	San Diego, CA
Age:	34
Profession:	Chief Executive of the Sperm Bank of California
Attitude:	As a non-profit organisation we make the dream of a family reality. We create and expand happy families according to ethical principles through donor insemination and sperm storage. These families have trusted friends by their side to achieve pregnancies.

Appendix ⟫⟫

Planungsbogen:
Zeitlicher Ablauf der Prüfungen – Lehrer   Topic 1

No.	Prep. from	Time	Team	Topic	Students
1a Minorities and Multiculturalism					
1					1.
2	7.45	8.15 – 8.45	1	The Best Exotic Marigold Hotel	2.
3					3.
4					1.
5	8.15	8.45 – 9.15	2	The Lunchbox	2.
6					3.
7					1.
8	8.45	9.15 – 9.45	3	Outsourced	2.
9					3.
1b Minorities and Multiculturalism					
10					1.
11	10.15	10.45 – 11.15	1	Bend It Like Beckham	2.
12					3.
13					1.
14	10.45	11.15 – 11.45	2	Bhaji on the Beach	2.
15					3.
16					1.
17	11.15	11.45 – 12.15	3	Brick Lane	2.
18					3.
1c Minorities and Multiculturalism					
19					1.
20	13.30	14.00 – 14.30	1	Gandhi	2.
21					3.
22					1.
23	14.00	14.30 – 15.00	2	A Passage to India	2.
24					3.
25					1.
26	14.30	15.00 – 15.30	3	Midnight's Children	2.
27					3.

Planungsbogen: Zeitlicher Ablauf der Prüfungen – Lehrer Topic 2

No.	Prep. from	Time	Team	Topic	Students
2a Challenges and Opportunities					
1					1.
2	7.45	8.15 – 8.45	1	George W. Bush: Address to the Nation	2.
3					3.
4					1.
5	8.15	8.45 – 9.15	2	John F. Kennedy: Moon Shot	2.
6					3.
7					1.
8	8.45	9.15 – 9.45	3	Bill Clinton: Second Inaugural Address	2.
9					3.
2b Changes and Challenges					
10					1.
11	10.15	10.45 – 11.15	1	Barack Obama: Speech in New Hampshire	2.
12					3.
13					1.
14	10.45	11.15 – 11.45	2	John F. Kennedy: We Choose to Go to the Moon	2.
15					3.
16					1.
17	11.15	11.45 – 12.15	3	Ronald Reagan: Second Inaugural Address	2.
18					3.
2c War and Prayer					
19					1.
20	13.30	14.00 – 14.30	1	Rudolph W. Giuliani: Speech at the Prayer Service	2.
21					3.
22					1.
23	14.00	14.30 – 15.00	2	George W. Bush: A Great People	2.
24					3.
25					1.
26	14.30	15.00 – 15.30	3	George W. Bush: Second Inaugural Address	2.
27					3.

Planungsbogen:
Zeitlicher Ablauf der Prüfungen – Lehrer   Topic 3

No.	Prep. from	Time	Team	Topic	Students
3a Global Trade, Modern Slavery and Migration					
1					1.
2	7.45	8.15 – 8.45	1	Jason Burke: Bangladesh Garment Workers	2.
3					3.
4					1.
5	8.15	8.45 – 9.15	2	Christian Parenti: Chocolate's Bittersweet Economy	2.
6					3.
7					1.
8	8.45	9.15 – 9.45	3	German Public Opinion on Refugees Is Turning	2.
9					3.
3b Going Hot and Cold – Environment vs. Resources					
10					1.
11	10.15	10.45 – 11.15	1	Paul Braun: Global Warming Kills 150,000 a Year	2.
12					3.
13					1.
14	10.45	11.15 – 11.45	2	Nikhil Kumar: India's Needs for Coal-Fueled Growth	2.
15					3.
16					1.
17	11.15	11.45 – 12.15	3	Michael Meacher: End of the World Nigh	2.
18					3.
3c Terrorism and Migration in the Wake of Globalisation					
19					1.
20	13.30	14.00 – 14.30	1	Naina Bajekal: After Paris, Life for Refugees	2.
21					3.
22					1.
23	14.00	14.30 – 15.00	2	Maya Rhodan: President Obama and François Hollande	2.
24					3.
25					1.
26	14.30	15.00 – 15.30	3	Jared Diamond: Lessons from Lost Worlds	2.
27					3.

© Schöningh Verlag, Best.-Nr. 040159-3

Planungsbogen:
Zeitlicher Ablauf der Prüfungen – Lehrer   Topic 4

No.	Prep. from	Time	Team	Topic	Students
4a Utopia & Dystopia					
1					1.
2	7.45	8.15 – 8.45	1	Margaret Atwood: The Handmaid's Tale	2.
3					3.
4					1.
5	8.15	8.45 – 9.15	2	H.G. Wells: The Time Machine	2.
6					3.
7					1.
8	8.45	9.15 – 9.45	3	Matt Haig: Echo Boy	2.
9					3.
4b Utopia & Dystopia					
10					1.
11	10.15	10.45 – 11.15	1	Margaret Atwood: The Handmaid's Tale	2.
12					3.
13					1.
14	10.45	11.15 – 11.45	2	George Orwell: Nineteen Eighty-Four	2.
15					3.
16					1.
17	11.15	11.45 – 12.15	3	Ben Peek: Black Sheep	2.
18					3.
4c Utopia & Dystopia					
19					1.
20	13.30	14.00 – 14.30	1	Aldous Huxley: Brave New World	2.
21					3.
22					1.
23	14.00	14.30 – 15.00	2	Suzanne Collins: The Hunger Games	2.
24					3.
25					1.
26	14.30	15.00 – 15.30	3	Ray Bradbury: Fahrenheit 451	2.
27					3.

Planungsbogen:
Zeitlicher Ablauf der Prüfungen – Schüler

No.	Prep. from	Time	Team	Students
1				1.
2	7.45	8.15 – 8.45	1	2.
3				3.
4				1.
5	8.15	8.45 – 9.15	2	2.
6				3.
7				1.
8	8.45	9.15 – 9.45	3	2.
9				3.
10				1.
11	10.15	10.45 – 11.15	1	2.
12				3.
13				1.
14	10.45	11.15 – 11.45	2	2.
15				3.
16				1.
17	11.15	11.45 – 12.15	3	2.
18				3.
19				1.
20	13.30	14.00 – 14.30	1	2.
21				3.
22				1.
23	14.00	14.30 – 15.00	2	2.
24				3.
25				1.
26	14.30	15.00 – 15.30	3	2.
27				3.

Bewertungsraster: Mündliche Kommunikationsprüfungen – Sekundarstufe II

Name: _____

Prüfungsteil 1: Zusammenhängendes Sprechen

Inhaltliche Leistung/Aufgabenerfüllung		Begründung/Stichworte
10	☐	
9	☐ Die Aufgaben werden **ausführlich** und **präzise** erfüllt, wobei tiefer gehende **differenzierte** Kenntnisse deutlich werden.	
8	☐	
7	☐ Es werden **durchgängig sachgerechte** und **aufgabengemäße** Gedanken geliefert, die den behandelten Themenbereich auch erweitern können.	
6	☐	
5	☐ Die Ausführungen sind hinsichtlich Plausibilität und Argumentation **nachvollziehbar.** Die entwickelten Ideen beziehen sich auf die Aufgaben/Dokumente und beruhen auf einem angemessenen Maß an **Sachwissen.**	
4	☐	
3	☐ Nur **wenige** der geforderten **Aspekte** bezüglich der Aufgaben werden erkannt und richtig angegeben. Die Ausführungen beziehen sich nur **eingeschränkt** auf die Aufgaben und sind manchmal unklar.	
2	☐	
1	☐ Die Ausführungen zeigen, dass die Aufgabenstellung/die Vorlagen **nicht verstanden** wurden. Auch durch zusätzliche Impulse werden nur **lückenhafte** Beiträge geliefert.	
0	☐	
	Die Punkte 0, 2, 4, 6, 8 und 10 werden nicht durch Deskriptoren definiert. Sie werden verwendet, wenn die Leistung nicht eindeutig einer Punktzahl mit Deskriptor zuzuordnen ist.	

Sprachliche Leistung/Darstellungsleistung

Die Bewertung erfolgt orientiert an den in den Lehrplänen ausgewiesenen Referenzniveaus des Gemeinsamen europäischen Referenzrahmens (GeR).

	Kommunikative Strategie/Präsentationskompetenz	Verfügbarkeit von sprachlichen Mitteln und sprachliche Korrektheit		
		Aussprache/Intonation	Wortschatz	Grammatische Strukturen
4	☐ gedanklich stringent; effizient; klar und flüssig; weitgehend freier Vortrag		☐ präziser, differenzierter und variabler Wortschatz	☐ breites und differenziertes Repertoire an Strukturen; nahezu fehlerfrei
3	☐ vorwiegend kohärent und strukturiert; der Darstellungssituation angemessen; in der Regel sicher und flüssig	☐ klare, korrekte Aussprache und Intonation; Betonung/Intonation wird kommunikativ geschickt eingesetzt	☐ überwiegend treffende Formulierungen; z. T. idiomatische Wendungen	☐ gefestigtes Repertoire grundlegender Strukturen; weitgehend frei von Verstößen; Selbstkorrektur vorhanden
2	☐ grundlegende Struktur erkennbar; z. T. verkürzend und/oder weitschweifend; nicht durchgehend flüssig	☐ im Allgemeinen klare und korrekte Aussprache und Intonation	☐ einfacher, aber angemessener Wortschatz; Überwindung von Schwierigkeiten durch Umschreibungen	☐ Repertoire grundlegender Strukturen verfügbar; z. T. fehlerhaft
1	☐ sehr unselbständig, unstrukturiert; Zusammenhang kaum zu erkennen; stockend und unsicher	☐ Mangel an Deutlichkeit und Klarheit; Aussprachefehler beeinträchtigen Verständnis	☐ sehr einfacher und lückenhafter Wortschatz; häufige Wiederholungen	☐ auch grundlegende Strukturen nicht durchgängig verfügbar
0	☐	☐	☐	☐

Punktzahl Prüfungsteil 1: Inhalt _____ /10 Pkt. + Darstellungsleistung _____ / 15 Pkt. = _____ / **25 Pkt.**

Prüfungsteil 2: An Gesprächen teilnehmen

Name: _____

Inhaltliche Leistung/Aufgabenerfüllung | Begründung/Stichworte

Punkte	Inhaltliche Leistung/Aufgabenerfüllung
10	☐
9	☐ Die Aufgaben werden **ausführlich** und **präzise** erfüllt, wobei tiefer gehende **differenzierte** Kenntnisse deutlich werden.
8	☐
7	☐ Es werden **durchgängig sachgerechte** und **aufgabengemäße** Gedanken geliefert, die den behandelten Themenbereich auch erweitern können.
6	☐
5	☐ Die Ausführungen sind hinsichtlich Plausibilität und Argumentation **nachvollziehbar.** Die entwickelten Ideen beziehen sich auf die Aufgaben/Dokumente und beruhen auf einem angemessenen Maß an **Sachwissen.**
4	☐
3	☐ Nur **wenige** der geforderten **Aspekte** bezüglich der Aufgaben werden erkannt und richtig angegeben. Die Ausführungen beziehen sich nur **eingeschränkt** auf die Aufgaben und sind manchmal unklar.
2	☐
1	☐ Die Ausführungen zeigen, dass die Aufgabenstellung/die Vorlagen **nicht verstanden** wurden. Auch durch zusätzliche Impulse werden nur **lückenhafte** Beiträge geliefert.
0	☐ Die Punkte 0, 2, 4, 6, 8 und 10 werden nicht durch Deskriptoren definiert. Sie werden verwendet, wenn die Leistung nicht eindeutig einer Punktzahl mit Deskriptor zuzuordnen ist.

Sprachliche Leistung/Darstellungsleistung

Die Bewertung erfolgt orientiert an den in den Lehrplänen ausgewiesenen Referenzniveaus des Gemeinsamen europäischen Referenzrahmens (GeR).

	Kommunikative Strategie/Diskurskompetenz	Verfügbarkeit von sprachlichen Mitteln und sprachliche Korrektheit		
		Aussprache/Intonation	Wortschatz	Grammatische Strukturen
4	☐ flexible, situations-angemessene und adressatengerechte Interaktion; durchgängiges Aufrechterhalten der Kommunikation		☐ präziser, differenzierter und variabler Wortschatz	☐ breites und differenziertes Repertoire an Strukturen; nahezu fehlerfrei
3	☐ weitgehend flexible Interaktion; in der Regel sicher, situations-angemessen und adressatengerecht	☐ klare, korrekte Aussprache und Intonation; Betonung/Intonation wird kommunikativ geschickt eingesetzt	☐ überwiegend treffende Formulierungen; z.T. idiomatische Wendungen	☐ gefestigtes Repertoire grundlegender Strukturen; weitgehend frei von Verstößen; Selbstkorrektur vorhanden
2	☐ gelegentlich stockende und unsichere Kommunikation; Hilfe wird u.U. benötigt; Reaktion auf Nachfragen; weitgehend flexibel; weitgehend angemessener Adressatenbezug	☐ im Allgemeinen klare und korrekte Aussprache und Intonation	☐ einfacher, aber angemessener Wortschatz; Überwindung von Schwierigkeiten durch Umschreibungen	☐ Repertoire grundlegender Strukturen verfügbar; z.T. fehlerhaft
1	☐ stockende und unsichere Kommunikation; Gespräch kann nicht ohne Hilfen fortgeführt werden; geringer Adressatenbezug	☐ Mangel an Deutlichkeit und Klarheit; Ausprachefehler beeinträchtigen Verständnis	☐ sehr einfacher und lückenhafter Wortschatz; häufige Wiederholungen	☐ auch grundlegende Strukturen nicht durchgängig verfügbar
0	☐	☐	☐	☐

Punktzahl Prüfungsteil 2: Inhalt _____ / 10 Pkt. + Darstellungsleistung _____ / 15 Pkt. = _____ / 25 Pkt.

Note: _____   **Gesamtpunktzahl:** _____ **/ 50 Pkt.**

Datum/Unterschrift: _____

Notenpunkte	15	14	13	12	11	10	9	8	7	6	5	4	3	2	1	0
Punkte	50–48	47–45	44–43	42–40	39–38	37–35	34–33	32–30	29–28	27–25	24–23	22–20	19–17	16–14	13–10	9–0

Hinweis: Eine Prüfungsleistung, die in einem der beiden Beurteilungsbereiche *inhaltliche Leistung* und *Darstellungsleistung/sprachliche Leistung* eine ungenügende Leistung darstellt, kann insgesamt nicht mit mehr als drei Notenpunkten bewertet werden. Eine ungenügende Leistung im inhaltlichen Bereich liegt vor, wenn in beiden Prüfungsteilen weniger als 4 Punkte erreicht werden. Eine ungenügende Leistung im Darstellungs- und sprachlichen Bereich liegt vor, wenn in beiden Prüfungsteilen weniger als 6 Punkte erreicht werden.

© Schöningh Verlag, Best.-Nr. 040159-3

Evaluationsbogen für Schüler

1. Die Prüfung (Organisation, Durchführung)

Die Prüfung verlief für mich … ● so wie erwartet. ● schlechter als erwartet. ● besser als erwartet.	☐ ☐ ☐
Die Prüfungsatmosphäre war … ● angenehm. ● unangenehm.	☐ ☐
Der Prüfungsablauf war … ● in Ordnung/strukturiert. ● chaotisch.	☐ ☐
Die Prüfungszeit war insgesamt … ● zu kurz. ● angemessen. ● zu lang.	☐ ☐ ☐
Die Prüfungsaufgaben waren für mich … ● klar und verständlich. ● mit einigen Mühen zu bearbeiten. ● zu schwierig.	☐ ☐ ☐
Es gab einen Prüfungsteil, der mir besondere Schwierigkeiten bereitet hat: ● zusammenhängendes (= monologisches) Sprechen ● an Gesprächen teilnehmen	☐ ☐

	ja	nein
Ich habe mich innerhalb der Gruppenprüfung meinem Leistungsvermögen entsprechend durchsetzen können.	☐	☐

Wenn nein, warum nicht? a) Die Gesprächspartner waren zu dominant. b) Ich bin eher ein zurückhaltender Typ. c) Andere Gründe:	☐ ☐ ☐

_____

_____

Im Vergleich zu meinen Mitschülern/Mitschülerinnen empfand ich meine Aufgabe/Rolle … ● vergleichbar. ● schwerer. ● leichter.	☐ ☐ ☐

2. Prüfungsvorbereitung

	ja	nein
Insgesamt wurde ich im Unterricht angemessen auf das Prüfungsthema vorbereitet.	☐	☐
Insgesamt wurde ich im Unterricht angemessen auf die Prüfungsform vorbereitet.	☐	☐

Die verwendete Unterrichtszeit zur Vorbereitung der Prüfung war …	
• zu kurz.	☐
• angemessen.	☐
• zu lang.	☐

Mein Zeitaufwand zur Vorbereitung der mündlichen Prüfung war …	
• größer als bei einer Klausur.	☐
• wie bei einer Klausur.	☐
• geringer als bei einer Klausur.	☐

Das hat mir bei der Vorbereitung gefehlt:	

3. Fazit

	ja	nein
Durch die mündliche Prüfung bzw. die Vorbereitung darauf habe ich mehr Sicherheit im Bereich „Sprechen"/„Kommunikation" bekommen.	☐	☐
Die mündliche Prüfung bzw. die Vorbereitung darauf hat mich insgesamt sprachlich weitergebracht	☐	☐
Ich halte es für sinnvoll, im Verlauf der Oberstufe eine Klausur durch eine mündliche Prüfung zu ersetzen.	☐	☐

4. Bewertung

	ja	nein
Die Bewertung der mündlichen Prüfung entspricht meinen Erwartungen.	☐	☐
Der Bewertungsbogen ist für mich klar und verständlich verfasst	☐	☐

In Bezug auf meine Mitschüler/Mitschülerinnen empfand ich die Bewertung meiner Leistung als …	
• zu gut.	☐
• angemessen.	☐
• zu schlecht.	☐

95

Conversation and Discussion

opening a conversation
You should always start a discussion with some kind of introductory phrase:
- I saw an interesting programme on TV last night …/ I read a fascinating article in the newspaper yesterday about …/What do you think about …?
- Have you ever thought about …/What would it be like if …?
- I was really surprised to find out that …
- Did you know that …?
- Do you mind if I join you?
- Excuse me, …
- (I'm) sorry (to trouble you), but …
- Have you got time to …?

expressing your opinion/giving an opinion
- In my view, …
- In my opinion, …
- As I see it, …
- To my mind, …
- If you ask me, …
- I am sure/certain that …
- I think/believe/feel that …
- It seems to me that …
- There should be …/ought to be …
- I would like to …/I wouldn't like to …
- It would be a good idea to … (because …)

making suggestions/recommendations
- If I were you, I would …
- The best thing would be to …
- You'd better …
- Why don't you …?
- How about …?
- Have you tried/thought of … (+ gerund)?
- You should/could …

including your conversation partner
Sometimes in a discussion, you may find that you are monopolizing the conversation, and you would like to know what your partner thinks:
- So what do you think, … (+ name)?
- How do you feel about that?
- What is your view on this (matter)?
- What is your opinion about/of/on …?

interrupting your conversation partner
Sometimes it is the other way round. Your partner is monopolizing the discussion and you want to have your say:
- Can I jump in here?
- Can I just make a point?
- Perhaps I can interrupt you there.
- I'd like to get in on that if I may.
- Do you mind if I say something on that point?
- Wait a minute …
- (I'm) sorry to interrupt, but …
- Sorry, may I interrupt you for a second …
- Sorry, but did you say …?
- Can I just say/add that …
- Yes/You're right/I agree, but …
- I hope you don't mind, but …

changing the subject
These expressions help you to bring in further aspects:
- (Oh) by the way, …
- Before I forget, …
- I just thought of something …
- There's something else I wanted to ask you/say …
- Oh, now I know what I wanted to say/ask you …
- I know this has got nothing to do with what we are talking about, but …
- Could I just say … (before I forget …)
- Let's also consider …
- While I think of it, …

holding the floor
Sometimes you notice that someone is trying to interrupt you, but you haven't finished what you want to say, so you try to carry on:
- If I might just say this.
- Do you mind if I just finish what I was saying?
- I'd just like to finish making this point and then it's over to you.
- Let me just add one more thing.
- This is my final point.
- Would you please let me finish (this sentence/ thought)?

returning to the original subject
Sometimes people stray from the main issue of a debate and it is necessary to get back to the topic:
- As I was saying, …
- (Now) what was I saying/what were we talking about?
- To get back to what we were talking about, …
- Let's get back to …
- (Yes, well) anyway, …
- Let's get back to the point …
- But we digress …
- Where were we before we got onto this topic?

defending yourself

If someone attacks you in a discussion, you can say:

- That's not what I said/meant at all. I was merely pointing out that …
- You've got that all wrong. What I said was …
- You're putting words in my mouth.
- You are distorting what I actually said.

expressing surprise

- I don't believe it/that!
- That's strange/funny …
- Are you (being) serious?
- Are you pulling my leg?
- Really?
- You can't mean that seriously!/You can't be serious!
- I doubt it/that/whether …
- Are you kidding me?

ending a discussion/a conversation

When you feel that you have effectively finished your discussion, that the conversation is not getting anywhere or that you have exhausted the topic, you can finish off.

- We'll just have to agree to disagree on that point.
- Further discussion is pointless, so let's end there.
- We've heard some interesting points/some new ideas, so let's stop there and go away and think about them.
- I can understand you better now, even though I don't completely agree with you.
- Well, anyway …
- Would you excuse me now, please?
- Sorry, but I've got to go now.
- I'd love to stay and discuss this further, but …
- It's been a very interesting discussion. However …
- Perhaps we can continue this another time.
- Look after yourself.
- Take care.

using fillers

- Well …
- Actually …
- You know/see …
- Let's see …
- I/you mean …
- Now let me think/see …
- In fact, …
- I wonder …
- The thing is …
- I see what you mean.
- Right then.
- Let's say …

expressing complete agreement

- You're absolutely right.
- I completely agree with you on that point.
- Precisely/Exactly.
- So do I./Me too. (agreement with a positive statement)
- Nor do I./Me neither. (agreement with a negative statement)
- That's what I think, too.

expressing partial agreement

- You're right up to a point.
- That might be the case/true.
- You could be right.
- You've got a point.
- Maybe that's true.
- That's true enough.

partial disagreement

- Do you really think so?
- Are you sure?
- That's an exaggeration.
- That's not necessarily the case/true.
- It's not as simple as that.
- I wouldn't quite say that.
- I can't imagine that.
- I find that hard to believe.

complete disagreement

Careful with this one! You do not want to make enemies, do you? Try not to be abrupt or too direct.

- That is definitely not the case.
- I'm 100 % certain of that. (disagreement with a previous negative statement)
- That's not true at all.
- You're quite wrong there.
- I totally disagree with you.

Oral Examinations

Oral exams are a lot like job interviews, so you can prepare for these in the same way that job applicants prepare – predict likely questions and practice the answers. In general, an oral exam is an opportunity for you to **demonstrate your knowledge, your presentation and speaking skills as well as your ability to communicate**. Examinations can be formal or informal, but in either case you must listen carefully to the questions and answer them directly.

The **formal exam** usually consists of a set of prepared questions and the evaluation criteria usually follow a right/wrong format. In contrast, **informal exam questions** are more open, answers are usually longer and evaluated based on problem-solving, analysis, method as well as communication and presentation skills.

Preparing for the exam

- **Collect all the material** that is likely to be covered in the exam and **try to predict essay-type questions** (i. e. questions that require a more complex answer and include a wider range of aspects. If you work with a textbook, you can use the table of contents to find possible topics.
- **Write down possible questions** on an index card. Then practice answering each possible question out loud.
- Make **a list of vocabulary terms and phrases** in connection with the possible questions.
- Then select three index cards at random (*stichprobenartig*). Pretend to be the tester and ask a question that **connects the three aspects together**. This helps you to make connections between the different topics.
- If you are a **visual learner**, you may want to draw images to boost your memory.
- **Turn off electronic equipment**.

During the exam

- Some oral exams begin with a presentation by the student. For an introduction, **give some indication of what the topic or problem is about** and why it is important.
- Give the examiner **your full attention** and look interested. Maintain **good posture** and **eye contact**.
- **Listen carefully** to the questions and make sure that you **understand exactly** what is being asked. If a short answer is requested, keep it short – if more detail is desired, give a longer response.
- Give yourself a moment to **think before you answer**. If you do not know the answer right away, feel free to take time to think. If you are able to use a blank sheet of paper and a pencil, take notes and/or draw the images you created as memory boosters.
- If you do not understand the question, **ask the examiner to reformulate, rephrase or repeat** it.
- If you cannot answer a question, **state directly that you do not know the answer** and go on.
- **Do not simply answer with "yes" or "no"**; demonstrate your knowledge by explaining aspects and backing up your answers with two or three key points or examples.
- If you are asked to describe, analyse and discuss a picture or cartoon, use the **present tense** or **present progressive** for your description. Describe the picture/cartoon **systematically** (e. g. from the foreground to the background, from right to left, etc.).
- If you need a moment to decide what to say, you can stall with formulations like "If I remember correctly", "That reminds me of …" or "If that is the case …", etc.
- If you are being evaluated together with a partner or in a group, **remember to interact with your partner(s)** and respond to his/her/their remarks.

Follow-up

- Reflect on your performance (e. g. where you did well or poorly).
- Note how you could do better next time.
- Speak with the examiner if you have questions on the material and/or your performance. Ask if there is anything that you should have answered that would have improved your performance.

Acknowledgements

Images

front cover: © John R. Rogers Photography; back cover: © Michel Setboun/Corbis; p. 5: Best of 9Gag; p. 6: Image courtesy of www.keepcalm-o-matic.co.uk; p. 8: © 2012 Twentieth Century Fox Film Corporation, PM/IN Fund, LLC and Dune Entertainment III LLC; p. 10: © 2014 Artificial Eye; p. 12: © 2006 ShadowCatcher Entertainment LLC; p. 16: © 2002 Twentieth Century Fox Film Corporation; p. 18: © 1993 Channel Four Television Corporation; p. 20: Film4/Optimum Releasing Ltd Artwork; p. 24: © 1982 Carolina Bank Ltd. and National Film Development Corporation Ltd.; p. 26: © 1984 Metro-Goldwyn-Meyer studios, Inc.; p. 28: © 2012 David Hamilton Productions; p. 32: © Signe Wilkinson Editorial Cartoon used with the permission of Signe Wilkinson, the Washington Post Writers Group and the Cartoonist Group. All rights reserved; p. 33: © Joe Heller/CagleCartoons.com; p. 34: © Steve Sack/CagleCartoons.com; p. 37: © Zapiro; p. 38: Tom Johnston/The Sun; p. 39: Cartoon: DER; p. 42: Mike Ritter; p. 43: © Bill Day/CagleCartoons.com; p. 44: © Mike Keefe, InToon.com; p. 47: © REUTERS/Andrew Biraj; p. 48: Banksy, Rickshaw, 2009; p. 49: © Picture Press/Stern/Gerhard Haderer; p. 52: © Alaska-Tom – Fotolia.com; p. 53: © martin_33/iStock; p. 54: © Greenpeace/Steve Morgan; p. 57: REUTERS/Darrin Zammit Lupi; p. 58: Euro RSCG Asia; p. 59: © interTOPICS/mptv/ddp images; p. 63: ddp images; p. 65: ddp images/Capital Pictures; p. 67: © WARNER BROS/Kobal Collection/FOTOFINDER.COM; p. 71: picture-alliance/Mary Evans Picture Library; p. 73: Umbrella-Rosenblum Films Production, Virgin Benelux 1984; p. 75: Copyright: The Spoils Card Game/Arcane Tinmen ApS"; p. 79: Illustration by Mondolithic Studios – www.mondoart.net; p. 81: © interTOPICS/LMK Media/ddp images; p. 83: paperback edition, 1980, Publisher: Ballantine Books, Illustrator: CREDIT: Barron Storey; illustrations Role Cards: Matthias Berghahn/Verlagsarchiv Schöningh

Every effort has been made to supply complete copyright information. Should such entries be incomplete or contain errors, we request copyright owners to contact the publisher so that we can proceed with the necessary corrections.